Arthur and Joshua begin the Walk Across South Africa

ARTHUR, PEACEMAKER

by Arthur Blessitt

BLESSITT PUBLISHING
Hollywood, California 90069

ARTHUR,
PEACEMAKER

ISBN Number 0-934461-02-3

Blessitt Publishing, P.O. Box 69544, Hollywood, CA. 90069

A ministry of the Arthur Blessitt Evangelistic Association.

ARTHUR, PEACEMAKER

INDEX

"We must let go of hurt lest it becomes hate and consumes us in the inferno."

Arthur,

Peacemaker

If you can't love the one that hurts you the most,
how can you love anybody!

To write about South Africa is to walk into the most controversial and emotionally explosive issue. Yet, I did walk there, fast there, and as I left, part of me remains there and I take their smiles, tragedies, hurts and joys with me for all the days of my life. The following is a true story. This is not the story of politics but something bigger - the Kingdom of God. During eight of the past twelve months, I have lived with and talked to more people of all races in more places in South Africa than any other person. Of this, there is little doubt. In all my time in South Africa: living, sleeping, walking and having carried the cross on foot through most of South Africa and having fasted and prayed in the streets for twenty-one days, I can make this awesome statement: "I have not received one word of hatred, not one word of antagonism or criticism. I have only received love, kindness and beauty." South Africa is filled with some of the most beautiful people one could ever know. I have walked among, eaten, slept, fasted and preached with the people of all the racial groups. Their love has overwhelmed me. This book tells of these experiences plus the message that was so welcomely received. There is reconciliation and peace around the cross.

Some facts about the cross in South Africa:

Walked with the cross on foot 1562 kilometers
(968 miles)

Carried the cross in the following countries:

Republic of South Africa	Bophuthatswana
Ciskei	Gazankulu
Kwazulu	Venda
Transkei	Botswana
Namibia (Southwest Africa)	Lesotho

Fasted and prayed seven days and nights:
Oppenheimer Park, Johannesburg
Town Gardens opposite City Hall, Durban
The Parade in front of City Hall, Capetown

General facts about the cross:

Began December 15, 1969
Walked around the world through 83 Countries
Over 37,000 kilometers (Over 23,000 miles)
Total 44 million 822 thousand 808 steps
Wore out 102 pair of shoes
Cross is 12' x 6' (4 meters by 2 meters)

Johannesburg

Seven Days Fasting and Prayer
June 24 - July 1, 1986

The government in Pretoria had declared a national state of emergency ... the front cover of Newsweek Magazine blared "South Africa's Civil War." All public meetings were banned, news press was under censorship, the eyes of all the world were focused on South Africa.

I picked up the big 12 foot cross that had been my companion around the world and gave it a pat. Joshua, my fifteen year old son, stood beside me. His eyes had a special glow of commitment and no fear. He shifted his cross on his shoulders and said "Daddy, let's go." The two cross carriers stepped onto the sidewalk in the midst of the high, modern office buildings of downtown Johannesburg. The city is over a mile high and known the world over as the city of gold for the rich gold mines that are located underneath the city.

What was our future? The future of South Africa? For now, all that I could do was take that first step. The rest was in God's hands. We moved off down the sidewalk toward Oppenheimer Park which was to be our home for the next seven days and nights. We had walked only about a block when a well dressed man rushed up. Tears burst from his eyes. He grabbed me trembling. "Oh, Oh," he tried to speak with a voice broken with emotion, "I am on the way to my office and through the traffic and crowds, I saw the cross! I saw the cross! That moment, the Lord filled me with His Holy Spirit and called me to preach. I shall leave my business and become a pastor. Thank God the cross has come to us. God bless you both." The glory of God was upon us in mighty manifestation.

"Let's pray," I said and then the three of us wrapped our arms about each other weeping and praying. He said that he must rush on to work but he would see us later in the park. This was the first drop of rain in the coming flood.

When we arrived at the park, there were some people there to greet us. I looked about for a place to put the cross and I noticed a low iron fence that separated the park from the pedestrian mall. I felt that was the exact place to lean the cross. Joshua put his cross down beside mine. There were some news reporters and a couple of television cameras. The park was crowded with people sitting eating their noon lunch. I greeted many of the people personally just before the big clock began to fill the city air with its chimes of twelve noon. It was June 24, 1986. Joshua and I knelt down to pray. What a team! Crowds began to slowly gather around as we prayed.

I had carried the cross in South Africa for almost four months from October 1985 through January 1986. After returning to Los Angeles in February, I became very ill. I had had a brain aneurysm in 1969 just before I left with the cross, which was again confirmed in 1984 and doctors stated that I was in critical condition. Now I was in great pain in my stomach. I had seen doctors in Los Angeles, Miami, London, Switzerland and Oklahoma within a six week period. Finally, I was in the City of Faith Hospital in Tulsa, Oklahoma. Paul Crouch, President of Trinity Broadcasting Network had taken me on the TBN airplane to the hospital. I arrived in great pain and got worse as the days went by. Test after test was made. Finally, on a Saturday night I was in such terrible pain, in the middle of the night the doctor was working with me. All he could do was try to kill the pain. On Sunday morning, I lay in the bed as Sherry, my wife, sat beside me. Christians all across America were praying for me, having been notified by Trinity Television Network, the 700 Club Television, James Robison, and Richard Roberts Television programs. Somehow, God had mobilized Christians by the millions to focus their prayers toward me. I knew God had a reason for all this prayer. The room was filled with flowers and letters by the box. Then I felt the Lord speak ... "Your mission is not finished in South Africa." Those words shocked me but I felt peace even as I felt pain. I looked about me, grabbed a pen and wrote these words: "Oh God, I don't want to die in a hospital room with cut flowers; I want to die on the road with real flowers growing. I don't want to die with air from an air conditioning but with real wind blowing in my face." I said, "Sherry, call the airport; let's go." We didn't check out of the hospital. We just left. A few weeks later as the airplane took off from New York toward Africa, all pain left and has never returned. I wrote these words:

> And now I fly away to fulfill my dreams
> To put my life where my thoughts are
> I cannot promise I'll return, only that I want to;
> The price may be too much for my flesh to escape,
> But I will not bargain with God.
> I smile...here I go.

Arriving back in South Africa after an absence of almost four months, I rented a car and drove to a hotel far from the city. I stayed in the room alone in prayer for three days. I needed to cleanse my mind, purify my heart, get rid of the U. S. culture, be filled with the desires of Jesus. I'm back in South Africa. Lord, where do I start with the cross? What now is your mission? I had already felt led of the Lord to have an Arthur Blessitt Street University Teaching in Johannesburg, Capetown and Durban. These were already set up. This is a training of people in how to be an effective witness for Jesus, helping Christians to help others to experience the new birth into the kingdom of Christ. Little did I know how important this training was to be. I felt I should go to Rhema Church in Johannesburg on Sunday night before my teaching was to begin there on Thursday. When I arrived, the people saw me and took me to their wonderful Pastor Ray McCauley. He was so excited to see that I had arrived. Their church is a huge multiracial fellowship that is moving in the power of God. The building seats over 5,000 people. As the Pastor was speaking, I was sitting on the front row. Suddenly, the glory of the Lord was overwhelming and I saw a vision of me sitting with the cross in the heart of the three major cities, fasting and praying for peace and reconciliation. As I sat there in the park, the glory of God was poured out and people were saved, healed and filled with the Holy Spirit. All races were gathering around the cross as one family.

I looked up. All around me and the cross, crowds had gathered...all races...one family. That Rhema church vision was now a reality in the heart of Johannesburg. There were tears in many eyes, smiles upon other faces and a curious eagerness upon the faces of others who were now gathering out of curiosity to see the cross, and a man and a boy praying in the park. I invited the people standing about us to join in prayer. Some began to pray out loud. Then for long periods, there was silence. Then someone else would pray, then I would pray. After the prayer I made a brief statement of what we were doing there:

"My name is Arthur Blessitt and this is my son Joshua. We've come to fast and to pray for seven days in each of the city centers of Johannesburg, Durban and Capetown. I have walked around the world for seventeen years carrying this cross through eighty-three countries. We've walked across South Africa and as we've walked we've seen people of every color, of every background gathering around the cross along the roadsides. We've walked in the city centers, we've walked in the country, we've walked in the desert, we've walked through Soweto, Crossroads and along the beaches. We've lived with the rich and the poor, have eaten your food and slept in your houses and I've seen all people gathered around the cross in peace, in love, in equality and in reconciliation. After walking in South Africa for four months, I returned to America but God spoke to me and said "Your mission is not finished in South Africa." So we have returned. I thought I would be walking again but the Lord said "Fast and pray for peace and reconciliation around the cross." As I look at your faces, I see representative faces of all of South Africa. I am not here for politics. I am here for something greater -- the Kingdom of God. My prayer is the declaration of the angels at the birth of Christ "Peace on earth, goodwill toward men." It is the prayer of Jesus to the Father "Thy kingdom come, Thy will be done on earth as it is in heaven". At the cross of Christ, the worst of man met the best of God and peace was made through the blood of Jesus between God and man. I have come with good news. God loves you. There is hope, there is love, there is peace, there is justice.

Let the love of Christ and the blood of Christ cleanse us from our sins and free us in the Holy Spirit that we may be one. We shall be staying here day and night without food and we shall sleep in this park. You are welcome to pray with us at any time and I am willing to pray for you also that your personal needs may be met. I am happy to be in this land. The Bible says "the earth is the Lord's and the fullness thereof." This land is not the devil's land. He can't have it in the name of Jesus. Some of you standing here may say, "Arthur, I didn't come here to pray for South Africa. I need prayer myself. I don't even know Christ. I need to find Him." If that is the need of your life to know Christ personally, to be set free from the bondage of sin, then I welcome you to know Jesus. I would just like to ask that those of you who want to find Christ today please lift your hands and I will have special prayer with you right now."

As I looked about at the sea of faces that had gathered, hands began to be lifted up. Almost half the crowd wanted to receive Jesus. I invited them to come closer and those who knew Christ to step back. For five minutes, I explained how to receive Jesus and led them in prayer as they were born into the kingdom of God. I asked them to go stand under a tree and there some Christians would meet them and help teach them and give them gospel materials. The response was overwhelming. I could hardly believe my eyes. People began to step up requesting special prayer for themselves. This went on and on as we continued praying. It was like I had been here forever. As the word spread through the streets people came to be prayed for and to pray.

Just after two o'clock in the afternoon, I looked up from prayer and saw Pastor Ray McCauley with Pierre de Charmoy. Pierre is the number one pop star in South Africa. He is a young twenty-four year old singer from the Island of Mauritius, and has recently received Christ as his Savior. We had met earlier and he had come to join me in prayer. We greeted each other with a great hug. South African Television SABC just happened to be filming at that very moment. Pierre and I joined together in prayer for South Africa. Suddenly, there was a huge explosion. The buildings shook. I could see debris flying not more than a hundred yards away. A terrorist bomb had exploded in a crowded Wimpys' restaurant. There was stunned silence for a moment. Pastor Ray, Pierre, my son Joshua and a couple of other ministers went racing to the scene of bloody destruction. I remained by the cross in prayer. I had been in such situations too many times before. I knew that they could handle the ministry with the injured. I would remain in prayer to fight the real enemy, Satan. Jesus said in John 10:10 "The thief (Satan) cometh to steal, kill and to destroy. I am come that they might have life and that they might have it more abundantly."

Everyone from the group had now run to help the injured. I knelt alone with my arms around the cross. As sirens made their wailing cry, I also cried "Father, I come to you in the name of Jesus and pray for the binding of the demonic spirits that seek to steal the joy of life and the purpose of life, that seek to steal the peace on earth. I pray that the demons be bound that seek to kill men, women and children, and destroy hopes and dreams, I pray against these forces of evil. I pray Lord, for those whose hearts are filled with murder and hate that You will change them as You changed Saul who sought to kill the early Christians and brought great terror upon the early church. He was converted and became Thy great preacher, evangelist. I remember Lord, how Moses murdered and yet he became a great prophet; how David murdered and yet found mercy and became Thy great servant. So too, I pray for these to be converted that have blown apart innocent lives." Tears poured from my eyes as Joshua put his hand on my shoulder and said, "Daddy, it's horrible. They even blew up a little baby. There's blood everywhere." I put my arm around Joshua.

We had been together in Beirut, Lebanon and had seen such things in 1982. I thought of how much blood and death my son had seen and he's only fifteen, from the time he was a baby in Belfast, Northern Ireland in that war, even to this day. Again, he whispered to me, "Daddy, I'm, sorry that this happened but if there's any place that the cross should be, it's here in the midst of this place. The cross should be where the people need the most. I'm glad we're here." We prayed for those who were injured. Soldiers and police were everywhere; police dogs were sniffing for bombs. Then, unbelievably, there was another explosion! This time, in a garbage bin outside the nearby Holiday Inn. More blood, more broken bodies. This modern city was being shaken by the horror of unknown terrorist bombings. The victims were black and white. These were crowded streets and restaurants. My heart was filled with overwhelming sadness and yet I knew that there would be no outcry from the world, because, that which would be condemned were it to happen in Los Angeles, London or Rome, is condoned and accepted if it happens in South Africa.

As I looked up, there was a huge crowd. People had come to pray. No one knew if there was another bomb, where it would be and when it would explode. There was no place to flee to safety but the cross was in the middle of their suffering and hundreds gathered. There was a deep sincerity that was indescribable, as men and women stepped up and said, "I want to know Christ." As Christians prayed all about, lifting up their country, weeping and seeking peace, there was a bond of love and glory and urgency around the cross and a recognition that the only thing that could solve their problems was Christ, because the root of the problem lies within the human heart.

* * *

The first day of the fast and prayer had begun.

* * *

The following events took place during the next seven days in Johannesburg. I will try to share a sample composite of events. If I shared them all, just Johannesburg would be a book! However, the stories that I share will be in sequence of days, one through seven, to give you a feel for what took place.

A few days before the fast was to begin, I noticed in the center of my left hand, that there was a deep, yet sharp burning sensation as if a coal of fire was dropped in my hand. The sensation would last for a few minutes and then would be gone. I didn't know what was happening. Then, about a day later, the same thing began to happen to my right hand. Joshua flew in from Los Angeles to join me a couple of days before the fast began and as I told him about the sensation in my hand, I asked him to put his hand out in front of me then I laid my hand about half-an-inch in front of his, palm to palm. He suddenly withdrew his hand saying, "Ouch, that burns." I knew that it was the work of God but I didn't quite understand this unusual manifestation. The night before we began the fast, the bottom of my feet at the center part of the arch on both feet also began to burn. It was like I was baptized with fire and I could not explain what I was feeling. I told one man about it and when he felt the fire in my hand, he fell into my arms weeping for over an hour. As one middle-aged lady heard me telling another married couple, who were friends of mine, about what I was feeling as we sat at their dinner table, she said "I am not a Christian. I've never felt anything about God. Let me see your hand." When she felt my hand, she burst into tears and received Christ as her Savior. She is a very famous sports person in South Africa and the world, but I will let her give her own testimony so I will not give her name.

The manifestation of the glory of God in the park was so awesome. The healings began like this: I was praying and talking to people on that first afternoon. It was about two hours after the bombings when suddenly a lady rushed up to me weeping and smiling. "What is this? What has happened?" I said, "What do you mean?" She said, "I have been sick for years. I've been to the doctor today. I was walking along the pedestrian mall right there in great pain. Suddenly, I was completely healed. I'm in perfect health. I have no pain! I stopped, looked around, and I saw that cross! What is happening?" The lady was in complete shock and in perfect health as I explained our mission, prayed with her and she received Christ. She went on her way rejoicing saying, "I'm going to send my sick friends to this park." She was never prayed for, she was healed by the sovereign work of God. When people saw and heard this, another lady stepped out of the crowd. She was crippled with arthritis in her knees, elbows and fingers. She said, "Pray for me." Now, basically, I am an evangelist having walked around the world preaching. I have seen the outpouring of healing mostly for a matter of hours, the longest outpouring was ten days, but for me, this is not a normal occurrence. I believe in the healing power of Christ but I have not regularly seen this on a daily or even monthly basis. So I was normally as shocked as the person healed to see this series of astounding physical miracles. I prayed for this lady. Now, often when people pray for the sick, they get loud, or long, or very dramatic. But my relationship with Jesus is as a friend to a Friend (John 15:15); I know that He hears my prayers so I resolved to pray either silently or with only a whisper. My belief is that loudness is not necessarily more persuasive with God and I decided not to make the prayers very long. God can do something in a moment. And, thirdly, as has been my custom in the past, I don't try to make anything abnormally dramatic out of the healing itself. I don't need to prove God. He is. That is irrefutable. But simply to let the healings be a part of the normal everyday workings of God because the true evidence of a person's healing is that their family and friends know it. Yet, to make a long story short, this lady was completely healed.

At about ten o'clock at night, a large crowd was gathered in prayer. A man tapped me on the shoulder and said, "Would you help this lady?" There stood a lovely black lady sobbing. I said "Ma'am, what is your problem?" There in front of all the people, she said, "My two brothers have just been burned to death by necking." Now, "necking" is the new vicious and horrible way of terror that is taking place in many of the black areas. In order to intimidate those who are working at jobs, who may be paying their rent, or who will not join in violence, or who hold any position of responsibility, or in any way are branded as cooperative with the government, authority, or business, sometimes mobs of teen-agers or young men will take a person from their house or their car, put an automobile tire over them with their hands and body jammed inside the tire, pour gasoline on them in the tire, and set them on fire. This is the form that many of the killings in South Africa take. Her two brothers, who had families, had been burned to death this way that night. Someone had told her in the afternoon that they had seen a man with a big cross that was going to be staying in Oppenheimer Park. Upon hearing of the deaths of her two brothers, she said to her friends, "Take me to the cross, take me to that man with the cross. I need prayer." The entire crowd was weeping. Pierre de Charmoy, South Africa's most popular singer, was sitting in the crowd without his guitar. I was holding the lady in my arms. I turned to Pierre and said, "Dear lady, Pierre is going to sing to you, just you. We want you to know we love you and Jesus loves you;" and Pierre, choking with tears, sang her one of the most beautiful songs I have ever heard. She prayed and welcomed Christ into her life as her Savior and Lord. She even left with a smile. She came back again and again during the next week.

As the cross was leaned against the low iron fence, it became the headrest for my bed. My bed was a sleeping bag on the cold ground. Many people picture Africa as being tropical heat with hot, humid nights, which it is north of here and also during the summertime, but this is South Africa and the summertime in the northern hemisphere is wintertime in the southern hemisphere. This is the height of the winter. The nights and most days are very cold. Johannesburg is over a mile high. The nights are usually about freezing temperature from one to four degrees celsius and the daytime from fifteen to twenty-three degrees celsius, with very strong, cold winds blowing. This means that I was, most of the time, wearing gloves, two pair of socks, thermal underwear, a cap like a ski cap that pulls down over the ears and often myself and the crowds were wrapped in blankets. At night, after midnight, a small group of us would lay down a plastic sheet and put our sleeping bags side by side in a row and sleep, or at least attempt to sleep -- people kept coming all through the night for prayer. In order for me to get any sleep, we tried to have a few people awake and praying so that they could talk to the people in the late night hours. As I crawled into my sleeping bag, with my head under the cross looking up at the star filled night, I thought -- there is nowhere better for me to be than in the cold, in the night, in a park, with the cross, in the heart of troubled South Africa. This is where the cross is supposed to be. Just as I prepared to go to sleep, Pierre de Charmoy arrived with his guitar and for hours we sang through the night. He would sing and then I would sing my Arthur Blessitt "road music". He said, "I like your songs" and I told him I liked his. Then we felt we should do one together. And, there, at four o'clock in the morning in the cold, after a day of bombing, prayer, heartache and joy, we wrote the story of our dream in a song that has now been recorded by him, with a video that we made, also with me singing (Ha!) called "One Family"....for that truly is our dream, as it was the dream of Christ in John 17:22 "that they may be one."

Second Day

Oh, dear God, it's glory! I sit in awe. It is total and constant people coming to the cross. I write about this day on the third day because actually, on the second day, there was not even one moment to write. I am completely exhausted. I have had no sleep now in two nights and two days. Of course, I'm fasting so I haven't eaten either. A great crowd had gathered and as we were praying, a drunk man came by. He was very loud and seemed almost out of his mind. Many of the people thought he was disturbing us. I stopped praying and said, "Friends, if you wanted quiet meditative prayer, you should have stayed at home or a church. The cross is in the middle of the city and in the middle of the city there are drunk and lonely people. My father had many drunk and hurting nights. Pardon me as I leave you for a moment. I'm going to take him over to the side and talk with him." As we sat and talked on a park bench, he reached into his pocket and pulled out an old beaten-up photograph and identity papers. He had been a military commander with the British forces during World War II. The scars of war were still ravaging his life. We prayed together and he left a new creation in Jesus Christ. II Corinthians 5:17 "Therefore, if any man be in Christ, he is a new creature: old things are passed away; behold, all things are become new."

As I sat praying and as others were praying, I was looking about at the crowd. I saw a lady and a man approaching us. The man was half carrying the lady as she was shaking and obviously severely crippled. I got up and went to meet them and we sat down together on a park bench. They had heard about the cross and wanted to come. They were both new-born Christians. She had tried to commit suicide sixteen months ago and the aftermath was severe brain damage, with difficulty in walking and speaking. Her hands shook uncontrollably. When I asked if she could write, her husband said, "No." He said only three days ago, she had to sign a document. By holding her hand, they were able to make an almost indistinguishable X. The Spirit of the Lord moved upon me to pray for her. I put her shaking hands in mine and slowly began to pray quietly as I touched her arms and her shoulders. Her hands became calm and her arms were no longer shaking and the Lord spoke to me that she's going to be a great writer. As I took out the pen from my pocket, I said, "Here, this is your pen. I want you to write me something." She said, "I can't write." I said, "I believe now that you can." She took the pen in her hand. I said, "write Jesus," and she did, as clear as I could have, and then she began to write more. She was so excited and her husband was ecstatic! God had performed another astounding work before my eyes. On Sunday, June 29, five days later, she and her husband came back. For the first time in sixteen months she could walk one hundred steps without support and she had written me a letter!

Third Day

A man brought a sheepskin blanket and gave to me so I slept last night after midnight and woke up at 5:30 a.m. feeling much better. I took a bath in a hotel room, but one wonderful thing happened. A pharmacist who has a shop only one block away gave me the key to their toilet, so now, we can go to the bathroom nearby.

Today was glorious, absolutely glorious! Hundreds and hundreds were converted. Crowds gathered without end throughout the day and night. Many Christians and pastors have now come to help. After inviting the crowd to receive Christ, someone takes them to the side for counseling. We now have interpreters in five or six local African languages as well as gospel material in those languages. Mr. Richard Scallan, my dear friend from Durban, came to spend the day with me in prayer. An elderly lady came rushing up to me, interrupting a conversation I was having with someone. "Arthur, Arthur," she cried, "I met you in Windhoek, Southwest Africa, in January. You prayed for me and gave me your book 'Arthur, A Pilgrim'. I love you, I love you. I have written to you and you have written back." I said, "What are you doing here?" She said, "I was visiting some friends here in Johannesburg and I read this morning in the newspaper that you were here. I came to see you." It was such a wonderful reunion. Then she said something to me: "I am deaf in my right ear, completely deaf and it's been that way for years. That's why I always turn my head when I speak to you. Do you think there is anything you can do to help my ear?" I smiled, laughed and hugged her and just put my hand over her ear and said, "Jesus, this dear, sweet lady who loves You so much wants this ear healed. Now I can only ask You as a friend to a friend. She's so sweet, Lord, if You will, heal this ear just as a special blessing to her." I was smiling and hugging her. She was so sweet, just like a mother or a grandmother to me. I put my hand over her other ear and whispered softly in what was to be the deaf ear, "I love you; do you love me?" "Yes, yes" she hollered. "I love you and I can hear you." She plugged up her good ear with her own finger and I whispered from far away. She was healed and I was laughing. "You must come to my house. You must come back to South West Africa. Everyone is waiting for you." She stayed with us for a long time.

While I was talking to that lady and other people that had gathered, a wonderful young lady and friend of mine, Brigitte Hupkes, was giving out gospel material in the mall area only a few feet away. A lady was sitting holding her child. Brigitte spoke with the mother, shared Christ and the lady gave her heart to the Lord. The three year old boy was still sitting in his mother's lap. After receiving Christ, the woman said to Brigitte, "Would you pray for my child?" Brigitte said, "Did you come here for prayer?" She said, "No, I just sat down to rest for a moment and I saw that big cross and now you

have led me to Jesus. Now would you pray for my son? He
is crippled. He has never walked. His right leg is stiff
and his right arm is stiff." Brigitte had never prayed
for anyone to be healed so she looked for me. She saw
that I was busy and the lady insisted that she pray. So
with stumbling words, she prayed for the child. The
child didn't move and nothing seemed to have happened.
In a few minutes, she came to me and said, "Arthur, I
just led a lady to the Lord and her son is crippled and
has never walked and she wants prayer for her boy and I
don't know how to pray for the sick. Would you please
come pray for this child?" I asked the people to excuse
me for just a moment and I went with her to where the
lady was sitting just behind the cross. Brigitte pointed
to the lady and said, "That's the lady and
that's---------" She stopped. I said, "What?" She was
speechless. I stood looking about for this crippled
child. All I could see was a small boy about three years
old, walking around. The mother was sitting there in
stunned silence and so was Brigitte - standing in
stunned silence. "Where is the boy?" I said to Brigitte.
She stammered in her speech, pointed her finger at the
little child standing alone and she said, "That's him."
I said, "I thought the boy couldn't walk." Brigitte
said, "He couldn't. I felt his leg. It was stiff." The
boy's leg was completely healed and he was walking but
his arm was still crippled. I took the little boy in my
lap, prayed for his arm and put him down and he stood
upon his feet alone. Then I held his good hand with my
hand and offered him a gospel pamphlet toward what had
been the crippled hand. He reached up and took the
gospel tract in his fingers. A great rush of joy and
laughter burst forth from all of us. Without any
announcement, as people had seen what happened, a huge
crowd gathered. It was absolutely unbelievable. Hour
after hour crowds came and every fifteen minutes to

half-an-hour, I would stop praying just long enough to invite those who wanted to receive Jesus to be converted and they were saved by the hundreds. We had to ask the Christians to call their friends to get more counselors to come and help.

Tonight there was a big crowd of people. There are so many people wanting prayer, and drunks that need counsel, it's difficult to keep control. It's just almost totally holy, glorious chaos. So many people wanted to spend the night until we had to ask some of them to please go home to their own beds because the park was beginning to look like a campground. I could not sleep all night. I would rest for awhile, but not sleep. Everything is too beautiful! The stars, the moon, the sound of the chimes of the clock every quarter hour, the people of all races and the quiet glory of God. If I had only lived one day, today, it would have been worth my time on this planet. Oh, I almost forgot! A couple got married this morning and the first thing they did was come to the cross and ask for prayer before going on their honeymoon!

Fifth Day

I tell you, it goes on. Just awesome! All day and night people coming to the park praying, weeping, receiving Christ, getting right with God, being healed. It seems like it is raining love.

At dawn this morning, there were over fifty people praying. The pigeons are a mess. Everywhere you look there are pigeons. This is their favorite resting place and feeding place. People throw bread crumbs on the ground and five hundred pigeons converge. The whole area is covered in pigeon squat and me and the cross and

Joshua, along with all the people, are camped in here with them. So many of the unemployed blacks come here in the daytime. Many poor unemployed and needy people are here as well as those of all races who work in shops and offices. It's very cold today. If anyone is making their bed with the poor, this is it. The glory of God is evident in an awesome way as the peace of God blankets this area. People say that when they step on these park grounds or come within say a hundred feet of here, they can feel a complete difference. The presence of the Lord is so evident.

Tonight a lady was walking by with no knowledge of what was here. She did not believe Christ died on the cross and that He was the Divine Son of God. But as she saw the cross and us sitting around it, God gave her a vision of Jesus in the Garden of Gethsemane and then of Him being crucified on the cross. We noticed her standing at the edge of the crowd weeping. We were all sitting down wrapped in blankets and heavy coats. I said to her, "Why are you weeping?" and she told us. I invited her to the cross. She kneeled at the cross weeping and received Jesus Christ as her Lord and Savior. She was gloriously changed. We gave her gospel material and a Bible. Someone offered to give her a ride home but she said, "No, I will walk home. I'm not afraid. I have my gun with me," and she held up her Bible. She came back often to visit us.

Yesterday a man came to me who owns a jewelry store. He was very excited and said, "Next time you need to go to the toilet, please come to my store. I have something to give you." Later that afternoon, Joshua and I went and the man gave me a beautiful gold ring with the word FAITH engraved in it and a cross on top. I thanked him for the gift but said that I did not normally wear gold jewelry and I could only accept it if I was free to give it away if I felt so led. Hesitantly, he agreed saying, "I know this ring is for you." The next morning after I had taken a bath, I had planned to leave the ring with my clothes but the Lord said, "Take the ring to the park. The man that the ring is for will come before noon." I placed it in my pocket. The crowds were all around the cross, people of all races, but suddenly, one tall, handsome, black man with his wife and infant baby caught my special attention. "This is the man that you are to give the ring to", I felt the Lord whisper. I went to him and we began to talk. He had come from the north of South Africa in the black homeland of Gazankulu from a town called Giyani. He had heard about the cross and the man praying and they had come to see me. When he told me where he lived, I said, "That's near Venda and I feel that God wants me to carry the cross up there." The man got so excited. "Come to me. I will walk with you. You can preach at our church. You can stay at my house." Then he stopped abruptly, looked at me and said hesitantly, "Do you sleep in black people's houses?" Looking him straight in the eye, I said, "No", pausing for a moment. He stood in silence. Then I spoke, "I stay in people's houses. I don't care what their color. At the end of the day, I sleep with the people that I'm among whether they are Chinese, Indian, European, African or whatever color." He grabbed me and gave me a big hug and his wife said, "You will sleep in our bed." Then I said to him, "Will you give me your hand? I have something special for you. You can do with it as you will. Keep it, give it away, or sell it." Then I placed the ring on his little finger which was a perfect fit. He could not speak. I said, "I'll see you in Giyani in August." The rest of the story will be told later in the book. His name was Piet Mabunda.

Gustar Mnguni, a black lady, has become my dear friend and companion. She was here in the park the first day we arrived. She was so dirty, it's impossible to describe. Her poor condition was beyond words. But she received Christ as her Savior that day as Peter Rahme, a local evangelist who is helping me here, prayed and counseled with her. She has been spending her days and nights here. If people tried to give me money, I would say, "No, I don't take money, but you can give it to that lady over there." Soon she was in clean clothes and well dressed. She was a new person. Her smile was one of the most radiant I've ever seen. She was planning to go to church tomorrow and yet I saw that her shoes were only rubber from an automobile tire tube wrapped with string. I had one of the Christian young ladies take her to a shoe store and buy her some new shoes. She is so beautiful inside and out. She has become like a sister to me. She keeps the place clean, keeps all our gospel material in order, shares Christ with everybody and is a powerful witness. A well-dressed man came by this afternoon. He looked at her and said, "Is that really you?" She began to laugh. He looked at me and said, "Why, this woman is a very famous singer here. She has sung in the best night clubs and has also been a great actress in the theater." She looked at him and said, "Jesus picked me up from the dirt," and she smiled. She is now active in church and is singing in a gospel band at the huge Rhema Church in Johannesburg.

It's unbelievable. I brought several hundred dollars here to give out to the poor and needy and yet after five days, I have more money than I started with. I turn away the gifts but people keep sticking money in my pockets, or laying it beside the cross. I keep giving it away and it keeps accumulating. What a blessing to be a funnel of help to those in need. One of the greatest needs every day and night is the people who have no jobs. It breaks your heart when people ask you to pray for them to find work. One man was walking by today and heard me praying for people to be able to get a job, for God to heal and bless the economy so that there is work for people, good wages so they may have the personal dignity of a job. The man came up. I prayed with him to receive Christ. He said, "Now Jesus will go with me and help me to find a job." He came back tonight to say, "Thank you. I've been without a job for five years. Now I have work. I'm laying carpet. I can now face my wife and children. Oh, thank You Jesus."

Tonight, I saw one of the most glorious things that anybody could ever see. There was a group of soldiers in uniform who were called up from the Reserves during the state of emergency. They are on active duty doing patrols in the huge black township of Soweto with approximately one-and-a-half million inhabitants. These young men are deeply committed to Christ and I had met them in a church about two weeks ago. Around the cross were people from all over the greater Johannesburg area and there were many blacks who lived in Soweto, who were deeply committed to Christ and were there praying. Somehow, the white soldiers and the black residents of Soweto met each other. They moved away from the crowd and I noticed this group of soldiers and blacks sitting together on the grass talking, praying together and smiling. After about an hour, I walked over to speak to them and discovered what was happening. They were together as brothers and sisters in Christ talking about their children and families. As the soldiers came to know these men and women, they said, "Could we all come over and gather around the cross and pray together for the healing of South Africa, for the end of hate, death and injustice, for understanding, love and peace?

Because of Christ and the cross, we are one family." We gathered around the cross together. A great crowd of people joined us. We were smiling and weeping and praising God. This is the hope of South Africa. This is the real South Africa. It's only a shame that the world could not see this picture as well as the other pictures. They exchanged addresses and all wanted copies of the pictures that I took. What a glorious day!

This afternoon, the glory was so great! For two hours, we could not have a prayer for South Africa because each time we tried to pray, the lost would speak up, "I need to find Christ." Hour after hour. Finally, I had one prayer for South Africa and then for four hours more, hundreds of people were saved. It is becoming impossible to pray for South Africa as so many needy and hurting people are coming to be prayed for themselves.

A Colonel in the South African army came to see me tonight. He said, "My men are so inspired with what is happening here, they all have your Jesus stickers. I just wanted to say thanks for coming to South Africa. Our country and my men are blessed with your presence."

The work of God's Spirit is almost completely out of control. Hundreds are gathered around the cross and at one time, I counted fifteen groups praying in the park as they could not get near enough to the cross to hear the prayers.

Sixth Day

I was awakened at 6:30 this morning by people wanting to receive Christ. About nine o'clock, a lovely girl named Isabel Pinto came by to celebrate her twenty-first birthday and for us to dedicate her life to Jesus.

Someone had brought flowers and put them on the cross. I gave her the bouquet of flowers. I can never forget her smile.

A mother brought her sixteen month old boy whose feet, legs, and hands were drawn up in paralysis. It was one of the worst cases you could ever see. I whispered a prayer for him. His legs straightened out, received strength and he could stand on his legs. One of his arms and hands began to work. The other one was still crippled. His mother and friends were ecstatic. All afternoon people came by the hundreds to be saved and healed. I'd say at least two out of three were completely healed. I feel very weak today but full of joy and glory.

Just a thought...The problems are so complex. It confounds the wisest of world leaders, yet so simple as a child - love and trust.

Seventh Day

This afternoon was unreal. A constant flow of people coming to be prayed for. It was so absolutely glorious! I prayed for people so long, I did not have the strength to stand. I sat down, leaning against the cross, and put a pad down in front of me. People came and knelt, one or several at a time. They were converted and we had people to counsel them. Others were healed. People are coming from miles around. I am completely exhausted. I have never seen anything like this during a fast. This is my last night here. Before midnight there was a small group of some of the regular people who had been helping me that were staying the night. I felt that we should have a communion and remembrance of our Lord Jesus, with the bread in remembrance of His body and the wine in remembrance of His blood that was shed for our sins. We had this powerful communion time together as we spoke, sang, ate the bread and drank the wine in remembrance of Christ who was also present with us. Since 1963, when I serve communion, I always have footwashing as Jesus did on the night that He served the bread and the wine. Afterward, He washed the disciples' feet as recorded in John chapter thirteen. I will explain more about footwashing later. But since the night was very cold, about freezing, a strong wind was blowing and we were wrapped in blankets, I thought and then I said, "Well, for the first time in twenty-three years, I guess we won't do the footwashing." Since no one else had ever had footwashing, they didn't seem to mind but I felt this inner emptiness that it just wasn't complete. I needed to go to the toilet before going to sleep. Peter Rahme, who was spending the night also, said, "I need to go with you." On the way, I was talking about how important footwashing is. As we entered the toilet and we were washing our hands, he said, "Well, here's water" and I said, "Do you want to have footwashing?" He had been with me all week, day and night and is a real brother in Christ. He said, "Yes, let's do it. I've never washed feet before and Jesus said we should." We looked about for a place to have footwashing. We discovered an empty package of Dunhill cigarettes that we opened up and laid out on the footrest of the urinal. He sat down and I washed his feet with toilet tissue. Then I sat down and he washed mine. We were laughing and crying and rejoicing. It was the most glorious and best footwashing of my life. Hallelujah!

Last Morning of Fast

This morning we had huge crowds hour after hour.

Massive numbers were saved but I will share just one small story. Last December, as I carried the cross out of Soweto, I met an Indian boy as I looked for a place to spend the night. He welcomed me to his home and there I had supper, met the family, and all received Jesus as their Savior. I parked the cross in their house and spent the night. The next day with many tears we said good-bye and I walked on. He lived in the town of Lenasia. This morning, he came to the cross. We were so happy to see each other. I discovered that his brother, whom I had prayed with, had been killed in an accident in January and Shawn Reshawn, now eighteen years old, was looking for a job and could find no work. He is now responsible for his mother. I felt such compassion to help him. I spoke to the crowd, told his story and said, "Is there some businessman in this crowd that will give my friend a job?" One man immediately raised his hand and Shawn had his first job. I also forced him to take some money to help with his family. My heart rejoiced at Shawn's employment but also broke at the blindness of a world that wants to see South Africans without a job and with no understanding of the personal human and emotional suffering that it brings. As the clock's chimes rang out twelve noon, we were gathered in prayer. So many people were crying, people were kissing us, loving us, and their faces I may see no more till we meet in heaven. There was sadness and joy as I picked up the cross with Joshua beside me. Seven days and nights. The Johannesburg fast and prayer was history, but a living history. I left my heart with those people and carried theirs with me. As Joshua and I walked the few blocks back to our room, we were excited about our first meal. It was to be Japanese Sushi. We put the cross in the hotel baggage room and went to eat. On our return, going up the elevator, there was a horrendous blast - another terrorist bombing! It had exploded not fifty yards from our door and just at the corner near where we had walked. Even in the midst of glory and prayer, the evil agents of Satan had placed a bomb in a garbage container on a crowded street full of all races of people. More bodies lay broken, bloody and dismembered. A grim reminder of what peace and love and understanding is up against.

Durban

Seven Days Fasting and Prayer
July 8 - July 15, 1986

Durban is one of the most beautiful cities in the world. It has warm tropical weather and is sheltered by high mountain ranges warmed by the Indian Ocean with miles of beautiful beaches along what is popularly known as the South Coast. The City Hall is a beautiful historic building with a one-block park of coconut palm trees in front. Beautiful offices surround two sides. The historic Post Office is there with its bell chiming each quarter hour. The home for Joshua and me was the Town Gardens in front of City Hall. We leaned the crosses against a tall palm tree with clusters of coconuts high above our heads. Pigeons and throngs of people were our companions for another seven days. When I had walked through Durban last November, the response had been powerful. Now we had returned, the word spread like wildfire and within minutes of our arriving under the tree, a large crowd had gathered as we prayed. At the end of the prayer, I simply asked if there were those who needed to receive Jesus. A dozen were saved. We prayed again for South Africa. After that prayer, I asked if there was anyone else who wanted to receive Christ. Approximately forty more were converted and I was there less than half-an-hour. This continued without end, increasing in numbers for the next seven days. The response in Durban was to become one of the mightiest periods of time in my entire life. I don't know how to fully give the story except to say that there was a constant flow of people all day and all night, and I mean, all night. I had no sleep. People praying for South Africa, needing prayer for jobs, for lost friends, for healing, for personal problems. I don't know how it could be greater. The love and glory of God blankets this place. The Indian population is very strong here. There are more Indians in South Africa than any place in the world except India and most live in the greater Durban area in the province of Natal. This is also the home of the Zulu nation and is predominantly an English speaking area, whereas Johannesburg was English and Afrikaans mixed.

Second Day

Today was unspeakable. You'd have to be here to believe it. No sleep all night last night. At 5:30 a.m. there were over fifty people praying. Then there was a constant flow of people till 12:30 a.m. I was almost dead. This afternoon from 5:30 to 6:30, with hundreds of people all around me, I lay my head in a lady's lap and went to sleep. There has not been one moment of silence, for me to even sit alone and pray quietly. About every hour, I try to get everyone to pause and I have prayer for the peace of God and the blessings of God upon South Africa -- for God to wash out from our hearts anything that doesn't look like Jesus and make us one by the blood of Jesus as we gather around the cross. Then the demand of people for personal prayer takes over. We have a great team of Christians that are witnessing, praying with people and counseling. But as the word has spread, people are coming by the hundreds in a constant flow to be prayed for. It has become almost impossible to function.

A woman came to me yesterday and asked if she could

be born again. I explained to her how she could receive Jesus into her life personally and we prayed together and she was saved. Then she brought her husband and he received Christ, and then they brought his mother and she too was converted. They are all from the Island of Mauritius. The mother had had a stroke three years ago and was paralyzed in her right arm. I prayed for her and she was gloriously healed, completely, raising her arm above her head, she could hold things with her hand. She was in total shock. They came every day to the cross while I was there and are great witnesses for Jesus.

The word spread and the crowds continued to flow. It was like one constant salvation meeting. Such glory! It seemed as if each time we finished praying or even before we would pray, that approximately half the crowd would be converted. I have never seen anything like this. In Johannesburg, and even here, I haven't preached one sermon but the conviction is so strong, all I have to do is ask who wants to receive Christ and they rush up. Or we finish praying and I ask people to receive Christ and they rush up. I give a brief explanation, lead them in prayer, then send them to the side where others counsel them and give them gospel material. Many times we have several groups as many do not speak English, but we have someone from each language group that can counsel them.

The manager of a bank across the street came this afternoon. He was well dressed in a suit and tie. He said, "Three of our African workers were prayed for yesterday afternoon and were healed. I know them. I doubted that this was real but today they are still fine. Two more of our workers came over this morning during the office break and they were healed. I am a skeptic. I'm not a believer but I do believe these people are healed. I make more money than all five of these African workers put together but they are now healthy and I am still sick. Would you please pray for my legs?" I said, "Sir, the most important thing is to know Jesus." He said, "No, no, I don't want to talk about that. Just see if you can help my legs." I didn't know what to do but pray. I prayed for his legs and he was healed.

Fourth Day

I wrote this on the fifth day because I had absolutely no time to write. It was solid crowds from before dawn until 3:00 a.m. when I finally got to sleep. It was absolutely unreal. Only God knows how many hundreds were saved. Over and over again, at least half the crowd was saved each time we prayed.

Last November when I first came into Durban, I was carrying the cross out of the city toward Zululand. There was a Hindu of Indian descent with his wife sitting beside the highway selling mangoes. They had a small four year old boy with a broken arm. As I approached them, Mark Bernett who was my driver at that time and had been baptized that very morning in the ocean, was talking to them. They were so excited to see the cross. The Indian people had welcomed me tremendously in India. The same response was true in Africa. They wanted me to come to their house which was nearby. They were absolutely in poverty. He had been out of work for over two years. He could not find a job. They had no food but she went to someone nearby and came back with a small bit of rice and a small piece of meat and they fed us eating nothing themselves. I didn't want to take the food but had to as it was so important for them. Both husband and wife came to believe that Jesus

Christ was the Savior and Son of the living God who had died on the cross and rose again. They received Him as Lord and Savior and were so happy. I prayed for the boy because the doctors had said that his arm at the elbow would remain crooked and impossible to move. As I left, I tried to give them some money but the man refused. I was weeping and said, "Your son is my son. Your wife and family are like my wife and family. We are brothers. You cannot refuse me to help your family in need." At my absolute insistence, he finally allowed me to give him a U.S. $20 bill. I gave them some gospel material and left with hugs and tears.

It was now almost eight months later. I heard a car horn blowing fiercely in the street beside where I was sitting with the cross. I looked and saw this Mercedes car pulling into a parking spot with horn blaring. As I looked, I saw this man whom I had met selling mangoes racing toward me with open arms. His well-dressed wife was rushing along following him. He cried, "Remember me? Remember me? You came to my house. I know Jesus. I saw in the newspaper today that you were in the park. I now have my own company. I have thirty employees. My wife has a business. We drive a Mercedes car and we have a new house. My son's arm is perfect and my boy calls you 'Jesus man'." We were all hugging and crying. I said, "I wrote to you but I never heard from you." He said, "That's because we moved." His wife reached into her purse and pulled out the same $20 bill that I had given him eight months earlier. She said, "Since the day you came to our house and brought Jesus to us, we have been blessed. We have never needed to spend this $20. I have even taken a trip to India to visit my family. We are completely blessed. You must come and dedicate our businesses to Jesus. There are crowds waiting at the factory to see you." The only time during the fast in

Durban that I left downtown, was to go with them to dedicate their businesses. When I arrived at the large building, I was greeted by people wanting to touch me saying, "This is the man that brought blessings to the Raj Naidoo family." He then silenced the crowd, telling the story of our meeting but saying something that I had never known before. He said, "We were selling mangoes so we would have enough money to buy gas to put into our old car. My wife and I had planned late that afternoon to put some gas in the car and drive with our son into the Indian Ocean and commit suicide. I felt that no one loved me and my family. We had no work. We had no food. I am an honorable man and we felt totally abandoned in this world. The only thing we could do was to die with honor. This man came down the road with his cross and we found a new life. Now you all know the businesses that we have. We only hire people who have been unemployed because I was unemployed. We don't take people from other jobs." I inspected his factory where they do steel work. People were working so joyfully and there were Jesus stickers everywhere. He said, "I have a meeting in two hours for a contract on the new hospital. Would you pray that I get that contract?" We prayed. The next day, he came back smiling. "I am hiring now more than one hundred new workers," and he took some of the men with him, who were in the park and had no jobs, to put them to work. The South African television filmed his story and he, among others, is a living testimony of the power of Christ to bring new life.

When we pray out here, you can pray any way you feel like praying, by that I mean you can pray looking up, with your eyes closed or open, you can pray with your head bowed, or with your hands folded; it's not the position of prayer that counts, it's the condition of your heart. That's what God's looking at. Normally when we're in church they say, "Would you bow your head and close your eyes." I think preachers came up with that for immature people and most of us should have outgrown that long ago, we should just be able to say, "let's pray." Because closing your eyes and bowing your head is something somebody came up with in order to try to make you forget the world and close in on your own world. In the bible they prayed looking up, they prayed flat out on the ground, they prayed standing up, they prayed kneeling down and one of the least common known ways we know that anybody prayed was with their heads bowed and eyes closed. Over and over they prayed looking up. I don't know how we got to having our heads bowed so much, but it doesn't matter because we're living out here in such beautiful surroundings that as we pray if you want to look around, praise God, look around and pray, that is okay. If you want to bow your head and pray -- whatever position you feel like praying in, you pray in it. Out here, you'll see a lot of people looking around. Many times as I'm praying I look around because God will show me a need in somebody's life, or I see somebody that I recognize. We will become a family after we've prayed for a while, then you'll find that without anybody saying Amen, it'll kinda just break up into conversations and you'll be chatting or somebody will be chatting. It doesn't matter, we don't mind you talking, just try not to get too loud, especially if others are praying. While we're in the spirit of prayer and as you meet one another in the name of Jesus, the family of God is becoming a fellowship and is being filled with love and you're falling in love with somebody else and that's the way it ought to be around the cross. We're gathered around the cross, we're praying, which is really symbolic for the whole nation to be gathered around the cross in peace and in reconciliation.

This is the fourteenth day we've been outdoors with the cross, in Johannesburg and here and it's only been peace and love and it's so sad that the world news isn't interested in the good news of all the beautiful people gathered together in love. If we were all out here fighting we'd be on the front pages everywhere, but God hears, and He is listening and that's who we're talking to. As we pray you're welcome to pray out loud, but when we pray let's pray to God and don't preach a sermon. Sometimes, some people are tempted to take a prayer and use it for a means of preaching a half hour sermon to us. Well we don't need to hear your sermon, talk to God. If we preach a sermon, let's preach a sermon, if we talk to God, let's talk to God. So pray and we'll join in together with you.

You don't have to feel inadequate when you pray; God knows your heart beyond your words to express! He understands what you feel - perhaps the best prayer you will ever pray is beyond words, 'but the Spirit itself makes intercession for us with groanings which cannot be uttered.' (Romans 8:26)

"Dear heavenly Father, we just thank You that we have the opportunity of prayer, we have that opportunity because of Calvary, because of the righteous life of Jesus, because of the divinity of Christ, because of Your sinless life and Your death upon the cross and Your resurrection and Your ascension. You've paid for our sins, You're the intercessor that is our advocate before the Father and we can come boldly before the throne of God because of Jesus. We thank You for Your promises that the effectual fervent prayer of a righteous man avails much. We thank You Lord that You said that if any two shall agree on earth as touching anything for Your glory, it shall be done. We thank You Lord for Your promise to open up the windows of heaven and pour out Your healing upon a nation if we will repent and humble ourself and pray, then You will hear from heaven and forgive our sins and heal our land. So we pray Father right now for the outpouring of Your Spirit across this nation and all over the world, because we know that the earth is the Lord's and the fullness thereof. We just refuse to allow the devil to take over the territory of God. We know Your promises where You said that You would spare Sodom and Gomorrah even if there were twenty people and then if there were ten, then if there were five, and Lord, we know if You'd be that merciful to Sodom and Gomorrah and those wicked cities, that You would heal this land because the people are standing in faith. Hundreds of thousands of people are praying and many are fasting and we're putting our lives into Your hands to ask Lord Jesus that You restrain the forces of Satan and loose the Holy Spirit and pour out Your Glory over the land. We've seen all the races, coming together around the cross and we pray dear God that that would be a reality. We can see in our mind all the leaders meeting together in the name of Jesus, in reconciliation and love to work out the needs of the land.

We pray dear Father, that those whose lives are filled with hatred and with hurt, and even tonight those who may be plotting death and contemplating killing people, we pray that their hearts would be changed, that You would bind the work of Satan because we know that Jesus said that Satan has come to steal, to kill and to destroy but You have come that we might have life and have it more abundantly. So Lord, we just pray for that abundant life to be poured out upon every person and in every life. We pray, dear Lord, in the name of Jesus for You to bless churches as they meet and worship You.

Bless the pastors, dear Father, that they would preach in power. Bless the beautiful people that are gathering together in prayer groups to uphold Thy name. Bless the people as they go to work. We just thank You for the beautiful privilege that we have to pray here, openly and freely. We thank You Lord, that the people are excited for us to gather to pray for the nation and we know that in the name of Jesus we pronounce blessings and goodness upon this land. And we pray, dear Father, that it would be a lighthouse to the world of the glory and the blessings of God. We thank You for all the good news that comes to my ear every day as people are telling me what's happening in their towns, and in their homes, and in their office buildings. So Father, with this confidence we declare that this is Your land and these are Your people and You will save our land and release the blessings of Your glory. We pray God for the economics. We stand Lord against the forces that would destroy the peoples jobs because, Lord, we know that people need work and are coming here everyday asking, "pray for me a job, pray for me a job." We rejoice because we've seen so many getting jobs. But Lord we pray for more: we pray for prosperity, we pray that tomorrow factory managers would say, "Let's expand, let's start a new building, let's go forward and put more people to work so people can have homes, dignity, food, health, education and the best of life," because we know God that You want every family to have a good home, You want every stomach fed, You want every person to be happy. We come before You with the assurance that You hear our prayers, and You answer them.

Father glorify Yourself. We just thank You for these beautiful people. Bless them as they gather with us. We pray, God, for anybody that may not know You, that they'll be converted this evening in Jesus' name.

Lord, we pray for these precious children, right at the front. In the name of Jesus we pray, God, that they'll have a beautiful land to grow up in, with peace, and without fear, with blessings and not terror. That every child will have nourishment and health and education, and most of all, the blessings of the knowledge of God within their lives that they may have equality, justice and opportunity. We thank You, Lord, that we can pray out here in Your beautiful church, with the stars, moon, trees, birds, wind, grass and the cool breeze.

Lord I thank You for the night, I thank You that You made the day and the night. There's something so special about the night. We know that You love the night. Many nights You went away to pray all night, and You spent forty days and forty nights praying and fasting and the night before the crucifixion You went out to pray in the Garden of Gethsemane and You prayed there so often, when Judas brought the soldiers, he knew where to come. You loved to pray at night, looking out over the city of Jerusalem and also the Sea of Galilee. Jesus, You love the night, and we love this night. It's a beautiful place here, the sound of the traffic, the bells that ring from the building, the sound of people talking, the sound of drunks sometimes screaming, the sound of laughter, the sounds of the city. We thank You Lord, that You came to save the cities, You came to save the countries, that You love the people in the cities, the lonely people, the hurting people, the sad people. Holy Spirit, if somebody is suicidal or depressed, we pray that You'll wake them up or just bring them out of their apartment and bring them here, that they might meet Jesus Christ. We thank You that You've called us to be prepared -- You said Your coming is like a thief in the night."

Fifth Day

Just as I was trying to get to sleep, about 1:00 a.m., over twenty young people arrived. They had driven more than a hundred kilometers. They wanted to see me and pray with me. I was so exhausted, but looking into their eyes, I knew I had to stay awake and be with them. We finally finished at 3:00 a.m., and I crawled into my sleeping bag to sleep. I slept about three hours, up at 6:30 a.m. Felt like I'd been run over by a train. Ha! Witnessed all day, one after another saved. People were crowding around.

One lovely lady, her name is Erni Moller, who came to the park very often and shared the love of Christ with many, brought a friends' daughter. The girl was thirteen years old. (She had been crippled by polio in her right arm and hand which was immobile.) We went to the side, sat down and began to pray together. The power of God moved upon her arm and hand, she was healed. Yet her arm was somewhat weak since it had not been moved for over seven years. I instructed her in exercise. She could raise her hand above her head, open and close her hand, and move her arm out. The girl was almost in a complete state of shock. I'll never forget one thing. I said, "Do you feel fine?" She said, "Yes, except my thumb. It won't move." I couldn't help but laugh. Her arm was fine, her hand, she could move her fingers and yet her thumb was frozen hard like her arm and hand had been. I took her hand in my hand. A small crowd had gathered around. I prayed for her thumb and suddenly, she could move it perfectly. She kept wiggling her thumb, and seemed more excited about that thumb working than anything.

I felt stronger tonight than I did today, but the days seem to run into the nights and the nights seem to run into the days with no let up. As I was sitting down to write in my diary, I noticed a man and woman. She wore a beautiful wedding dress and he was dressed for marriage. I walked over to them. They had been married that afternoon at three o'clock, had the reception and then came to the cross for prayer. This was so powerful and was quite a celebration of joy for us as I remembered how Jesus turned the water into wine at a wedding banquet.

Tonight as we were praying, a lady burst through the crowd and grabbed me. She was weeping, shaking, and she said, "I've come by five times this week but I never had the courage to speak to you. Now I must. I want to be reborn." And she wept her way into the kingdom of God. The stories are endless. I have so many friends here in South Africa that it has become like home. All the people, black, white, Indian, colored, they're all the same to me, such love, oh so lovely. The glory of God covers this place and it's such a wonderful feeling it's impossible to describe. There is such peace and love here. I feel so overcome with glory. God help me.

Sunday, July 13, 1986

God protect me from promotion, organization and ego. Just keep me in the streets. It's so beautiful here, and the needs are so great.

Here, where the cross is, crowds gather - more than we can handle, eager, full of questions, full of needs, absolutely overcoming us with the desire to pray, wanting us to pray for them, wanting to find Christ. As

I see what is happening here, I look at the world and think, why aren't the ministers in the streets and the parks, exposed to the real people of need and desperation without a shield? For many in the ministry, it's a one hour worship service. Then they greet everyone after and go to dinner. Much of the time, when I preach in a church, as I stay to counsel the people, (one hour, two hours, three hours) I notice the pastor is already gone. If it's a night meeting, the janitor is flashing the light to drive the people out of the building. Time is up. It's over.

Being out here in South Africa, exposes the weakness of the church, of evangelism, and so on. You only have to go and sit in a park in the city and pray and the people come by the hundreds and then by the thousands. You pray for them. They tell others, "Go there, someone will pray for you." They come and it grows.

I fasted and prayed once in Hollywood, California for twenty-eight days. Again I fasted and prayed in Washington, D.C. for forty days and nights; for three days in Belfast, Northern Ireland; and then here in South Africa. Oh, you can see how hungry the people are. In each of those places, just fasting and praying, we were overcome by the crowds of people. You don't need a building or an organization just to be somewhere and the people come if there's anything worth coming for. But where are the ministers? We have a lot of new converts doing the work that confounds theology professors. They're shaking the city. How is it that ministers must have a plush office to counsel in? The world is lost, the people are starving and the laborers are few. Almost every church meeting that I go to, someone says, "Oh, I'm waiting on God to tell me what to do." They say, "Do

you have a word from God for me?" Oh, Oh, Oh God! God's
children are so blind, blind to the needy and the
hurting and the lost around them. We don't want to be
inconvenienced by the needy. We want to have a
"ministry." Then you can start at a certain time and end
at a certain time. We don't need "ministry", we need
disciples of Christ. We need twenty-four hour a day
followers of Jesus. Yesterday, I was sitting talking to
a very needy lady. She had waited a long time to talk to
me as I had ministered to others, then finally I got to
her. As we began to speak, she was weeping. Then this
superstar, dressed up, hair in perfect form, with the
best jeweled watch and ring, burst into our prayer and
conversation. "I'm pastor _____ _____ of the big
_____ _____ church in _____ _____. I want you
to come and preach." He had no concern for this hurting
lady or for my time spent counseling, and caring and
sharing. For him Arthur Blessitt was the superstar, the
big name, the man of God who could fill his church, who
he could tell his friends had preached in his church. It
was all ego and insincerity. I said, "Sir, can't you see
I'm talking to a needy lady who's weeping?" He huffed
and cut off my words. "Oh, but I'm _____ _____ and
we want you." I cut him off. "Sir, you are a man of God,
can't you see this lady needs help? I can't interrupt
this conversation to discuss something else. Wait a
minute and I'll give you the same time that I'm giving
to her." He rose up with a grunt, almost fire in his
eyes, swirled around and walked off through the crowd of
hurting people. He was lost and blind to the hurting
of individuals around him and inconsiderate of the
feelings of others. Oh God, where are the people who are
available to the crowds? I sit and think. There are few
people that expose themselves to true public ministry.
Here in this park, every day from twelve noon to two
in the afternoon, if several ministers would divide

their time and be here to talk and pray individually with people, they would be flooded. But who wants people! I've been in the biggest TV, and crusade meetings, in stadiums and auditoriums from time to time, at conferences, on programs with the leading teachers, preachers, evangelists and ministers. I know what I'm saying. Not once, but year after year after year, this is how it goes. The ministers are staying in the best hotel. In the afternoon, most of their ministry people go shopping at the best stores - for little things. Then there's perhaps an early snack and then the chauffeur driven car picks up the teams and we go to the hall, the stadium or the studio by way of the back door, often with body guards or attendants. Then there are snacks and hors d'oeuvres and the personalities stand there chatting about everything under the sun, many times watching a ball game or some program on TV until somebody says "Program begins in five minutes." Everyone gets their last minute make-up and hair ready, and the program starts. Often there has not even been one prayer meeting and everyone suddenly becomes super-spiritual. They have every gift there is. Words of knowledge, gifts of healing, mighty prophecies, great sermons, (but where was all this during the day?) Along the street there were crippled people, they never stopped to pray with them. All day in the shops, hotels, taxis and airports, there were no words of knowledge, but now on stage, "Thus saith the Lord, God loves you. God is interested in your every need. I am His messenger." Wow! "Come forward." (Many times, half are counselors to help the movement toward the front). "We want to help you." Perhaps it's a short prayer. Perhaps it's a wave of a hand, or a touch on the forehead in a long line of waiting people, or perhaps it's off to the counseling room, but the great man or woman of God, they vanish from the scene. Aides hurriedly empty the building as the prophet sips coffee and snacks behind stage. All the program people gather and discuss where they are going to have their late night meal and fellowship. The crowd has had a thrill and sometimes, especially when the group is a music group, the crowd can even see the "personality" up close and can get an autograph around the record table. "But please, no real ministry here, we're only signing autographs. Why don't you see a counselor at the front, or come back tomorrow." Many of the greatest name Christian leaders live in total isolation from the 'people environment'. Our god has become crowds, TV ratings, and success. But who has time for people, real people? My heart cries out. In almost every place, the people beg me to stay, "Don't go." I look at Jesus in the crowds of religious hangers-on and in Jericho He saw Zacchaeus, a sinner man in a tree. Not phony, not seeking an autograph of Jesus, but just wanting to see Jesus. And Jesus left the crowds of self-righteous and went to this man's home and ate with the sinner man. People condemned Jesus, saying that He was a drunkard and a wine-bibber, a friend of publicans and sinners. A sinner woman fell at His feet when Jesus was eating. With tears, she washed His feet and with her hair she dried His feet and continued to kiss His feet. This was Jesus. He let her stay there. She needed His touch and she needed to touch Him. And He said, "Thy sins are forgiven thee for you have loved much." Jesus was never on a high stage or speaking in the great Roman arenas that were present in His day. He was lost in the crowds of children with runny noses, dogs barking, donkeys and horses braying, goats and lambs, dirt blowing up and sand, wind tossing his hair about, hands that had just blown their nose, that had been riding a sweaty camel or donkey, or had wiped their sweaty faces, or had been to the toilet where there was no toilet, or a leper full of sores; these were the people touching

Jesus. This was Jesus. Crowds found Him. He was in the streets, available. Where are His ministers today? In ivory covered halls of theology, in plush offices lined with $50,000 worth of books, with church hours that match the world - nine to five, with gospel operations churning out computer "personal" letters where your name is used in the letter four or five times to make you feel that "he knows you." Oh, where are You, Jesus of Nazareth? Where are Your followers? You said when the people criticized John the Baptist, "What went you out into the wilderness to see? A reed shaken by the wind? A man clothed in soft garment? Behold, they which are gorgeously appareled and live delicately are in the king's court. But what went you out to see? A prophet?" Theologians debate theologians. Why aren't they out here in the streets to discuss it in the parks, on the beach, in the ghetto, and in the war zones? No, they play theological games with other intellectuals while the world goes to hell!

I don't want any theology that I don't live. Call me simple, but this is my desire, I want to live what I believe. That's what I want to hear from the faith teachers. Mr. Faith says, "This is a faith ministry. If we don't hear from you immediately, we won't be on the air next week. Put your faith to work dear friend and give God (me) a check right now. Make that faith check out to Doctor Shame, P.O. Box 1, Rip Off, U.S.A." (God uses this address also.) Where is your faith, Mr. Faith?

Those of you who have a word of knowledge, I have a place for you to minister. Why don't you go to Beirut, Belfast, South Africa, or Europe and tell where the next car bomb will explode?

Where are you faith healer? I have just the place
for you. Not in a stadium (as you stay in a five-star
hotel), but get a four-wheel drive and go where there
are no doctors across Africa, then through South
America. Somehow, the healing power only comes from 7:00
to 9:00 p.m. at the auditorium and where the crowd has a
generous love offering. Why don't you take your crusade
to a park in Watts or downtown Los Angeles, on the beach
in Florida, or to the slums of Calcutta? You could save
millions of dollars in promotion and draw even larger
crowds, especially the poor. But oh, it would be
difficult to keep one's hair in style and difficult to
take up the love offering. And also, the drunks, drug
addicts, the illegal immigrants might also come. What
nice person wants to sit next to a bum? (Only Jesus I
guess). Oh, I weep today as I see the crowd gathered
around. Right now, as I write, I am weak, hungry,
sleepy, tired and need to go to the bathroom. But how
can I write this if I'm not willing to live it! I'll say
good-bye world, you get off easy, I have more to say,
but no time now.

Sunday afternoon, it was unreal, people coming to
the cross. I left Joshua in the park with both crosses
and I went a few blocks away to the Christian center, a
downtown fellowship that meets in an old movie theater.
The pastor, Fred Roberts, is a dear man of God and he
had opened their place for an interdenominational
gathering. This afternoon, we had a great communion and
footwashing service. It was absolutely glorious and
indescribable. There were people of all races from South
Africa; whites, blacks, Indians, coloreds. It was an
awesome crowd. Thousands of people overflowed the entire
premises. We sang choruses and worshipped the Lord as
people tried to get into the building. Finally, the
entire stage was flooded with people and Pastor Roberts

turned the meeting over to me. I stood there at the front looking at the scene. Tears were pouring from my eyes. And then I spoke slowly. "This is the new South Africa. This is the real South Africa. If only the world could see." I read from Matthew, the twenty-sixth chapter, verses twenty-six through twenty-nine. "And as they were eating, Jesus took bread and blessed it and broke it and gave it to the disciples and said, 'take eat, this is My body.' And He took the cup and gave thanks and gave it to them saying, 'Drink you all of it for this is My blood of the new testament which is shed for many for the remission of sins. But I say unto you, I will not drink henceforth of this fruit of the vine, until that day when I drink it new with you in My Father's kingdom.' To me, the communion time with the bread and wine is one of the most beautiful opportunities of worship, praise, and thanksgiving that the believer has. Here we were gathered together to remember Jesus.

Jesus had said in Luke chapter twenty-two verse nineteen, "Do this in remembrance of Me." And we were gathered in remembrance of Jesus Christ. As we distributed the bread, I began to speak of Jesus reminding the people of His body. His hands that reached out and touched the sick and the sinful. His lap where the children sat and He said, "Let the little children come unto Me for such is the kingdom of heaven." His arms, where someone like John lay his head. His eyes, that saw the multitudes as sheep without a shepherd scattered abroad, that saw the city of Jerusalem refusing to hear the message of life and He wept. His lips, no man ever spoke like Jesus. His words were the words of life. His head, where the crown of thorns had been pressed into His brow and the blood flowed down His face. His back beaten and scourged with the Roman whip but with His stripes, we are healed. His feet, remembering once He said, "I must walk today, tomorrow, and the day following" - His feet bringing good news. The body of Jesus. His hands pierced with the nails, His feet nailed to the cross. The blood of Jesus Christ cleanses us from all sin. As I remembered and spoke of His body, we were weeping. He gave Himself for us. We took the bread, blessed it and ate it. Then we took the cup remembering that Jesus took the wine and said, "This is My blood that is shed for the remission of sins." And I reminded the people that only through the blood of Jesus Christ can our sins be taken away. Jesus Christ gave His life for us. Without the shedding of blood, the Bible says, there is no remission of sins. And there at the cross, through the blood and sacrifice of Jesus, peace was made between man and God that we might have His peace within our heart and life. We remembered His death which brought our life and His resurrection. He's not a dead Christ, but our resurrected Lord. Hallelujah!

After we had received the bread and the wine, we did what Jesus asked us to do as recorded in John chapter thirteen verse two. "And the supper being ended, the devil having put into the heart of Judas Iscariot, Simon's son, to betray Him, and Jesus knowing that the Father had given all things into His hands, and that He was come from God, and went to God; He ariseth from supper, and laid aside His garments; and took a towel, and girded Himself. And after that He poured water into a basin and began to wash the disciples' feet and to wipe them with the towel wherewith He was girded. Then cometh He to Simon Peter; and Peter said unto Him 'do You wash my feet?' Jesus said unto him, 'What I do you knowest not, but you shall know hereafter.' And Peter said unto Him, 'You shall never wash my feet.' And Jesus said, 'If I wash you not, you have no part with Me.' And

Simon Peter said unto Him, 'Lord, not my feet only, but also my hands and my head.' And Jesus said, 'He that is washed need only to wash his feet, but is clean. You are clean, but not all.' For He knew who should betray Him, therefore He said, 'you are not all clean.' So after He had washed their feet and had taken His garments, and was set down again, He said to them, 'Do you know what I have done to you? You call Me Master and Lord; and you say well; for so I am. If I then, your Lord and Master have washed your feet, you also ought to wash one another's feet. For I have given you an example that you should do as I have done to you. The servant is not greater than his lord, neither is he that is sent greater than he that sent him. If you know these things, happy are you if you do them."

Most of the time in our present world we only have communion and never the footwashing. I've never understood that. When I was just beginning preaching, I was pastoring a church in the state of Nevada in America. I had had my tonsils removed and was in the hospital, and I was reading the book of John. When I read those words, I realized that I hadn't done something very important that Christ commanded. He said you ought to wash one another's feet; I've given you an example that you should do as I've done to you, and happy are you if you do it, these three things. I had tried to justify not doing it as I'd heard my professors at the university and seminary say that those words didn't apply, that they were symbolic. And I remember always wondering if that was symbolic, why wasn't the bread and wine symbolic? But suddenly in that hospital, I realized that the water of footwashing was as real as the bread and the wine of communion and I had never obeyed His command. And I resolved that as soon as I got out, I was going to wash somebody's feet. It was at a pastors' conference the next week and in a hotel room that night, I said, "I'm going to do what Christ commanded me to do and I'm going to wash your feet, I don't know how to do it but if you're still in this room when I come back from the bathroom with the trash can full of water and some towels, then I'm going to wash your feet." When I came back, every pastor had their shoes off and we had the most glorious footwashing that you've ever seen. Communion is our relationship with God. Jesus said, "Do this in remembrance of Me." We remember His body, we remember His blood. It doesn't really relate to those that are around us. Communion is your relationship with God and your remembrance of Christ. But footwashing is our relationship one with another and it followed one after another that night. Jesus served the bread and the wine then He put on the robe of the servant and washed their feet. Somehow it's easier for us to try to deal with God who we don't see with our eyes, than it is someone sitting beside us whom we can see. God is a spirit, but we are physical and our pride gets in the way of this scriptural blessing. With the massive crowd that had gathered, we wanted to obey the commands of Jesus Christ and wash one another's feet, because we are one family, we're one body, we're the body of Christ. It's not divided by race or language. The only way we knew to do the footwashing with such a large crowd packed in close together was to give out wet towels that you can buy in a can. So the ministers that were there gave out wet towels to everyone and I asked for the people to wash the feet of the person on either side. Everybody would be washing at least two people's feet. Then I said, "if the women have on stockings, we'll just wash their feet through the stockings." We had prayer and then we began to fulfill the command of Christ. It is a scene that will live with me forever. Here in South Africa, with a crowd that was a very representative mixture of all the racial groupings, (at least half the crowd black as well as a large group of Indians, coloreds and whites), people began to wash one another's feet and pray for the person whose feet they were washing. Footwashing is one of the few commands in the Bible with a promise attached. Jesus said, "Happy are you if you do this." And I've found that to be true. With footwashing, there's an overwhelming joy that seems to flood the place. People were laughing, crying and smiling, hugging one another, praying for one another. It was glorious.

I might add this, that in my own family, with my wife and our six children, the bread, the wine, the footwashing is perhaps the most important and unifying force in our relationship. Most of the time before I leave on a trip or if we're all going, before we all leave, we have communion and footwashing. When I come back from a trip or when we return we have communion and footwashing. Then our kids are washing one another's feet and I'm washing my wife's feet and the kids' feet and they're washing mine, it just seems to cleanse and purify our relationship. Everything that's not right vanishes away as we pray and remember the body and blood of Jesus and then express that love to one another. That really is the needed message of our church today, to remember Christ, to love Him, and to realize what He's done for us in providing us with salvation and the new life, and then to express that relationship we have with God with one another. The work of Christ is to be the servant of one another. If only we could exalt other people, we could make every person feel better than when we met them. If we smiled, if we said 'thank you', if we treated every person honorably and the love of our life was real, what a new world it would be. This is exactly the solution all over the world for every problem. Many times, we have great declarations, words, we have tremendous statements of justice and equality, but do we touch - do we wash the people's feet with our love and with our life in a personal and real way? As people were washing one another's feet, it was a holy moment. A representative section of South Africa by the thousands was together in the beauty of love. If we had had a riot, if we were killing one another, or hating one another, the news media would have been there from all over the world because the world press is in Durban. But because we were loving one another there was no interest because there was beauty instead of death and this is not a rare occasion.

One of the greatest things happening in the world is happening in South Africa. There is a mighty, powerful, glorious spiritual awakening! Multiracial. All the races, a unity, cooperation, but this is never reported, never spoken of. The government wasn't against us all meeting together. That Christian center is multiracial all the time as are many other churches in South Africa. This is never emphasized by the press that the people of all races love one another by the grace of God - we're brothers and sisters. Then the Africans began to sing a song called, "Amen." I've never heard anything like that song. Everyone was hugging and clapping and praising God. Most of the blacks were Zulus and they were singing in Zulu, it was an unbelievable experience. At the conclusion of the meeting, everyone was bathed in love, unity and the power of the Holy Spirit and I invited those who needed to receive Jesus to come and pray. A number came forward to receive Christ, to be prayed with and counseled with.

I went back to the City Hall where the cross was and there sat Joshua. He had remained. A large crowd was

the Reverend Fred Roberts of the Christian Center. Since I refuse to take love offerings, they wanted to find some way of expressing to me how they appreciated what we were doing in South Africa. In 1979, I had a gorgeous parrot in Central America. His name was El Salvador del Mundo. He spoke Spanish and was my traveling companion in Central America and it was a very sad story when he died in Nicaragua during the civil war. We had sprayed for mosquitoes and El Salvador overdosed on the mosquito spray and died and I wept, and wept, and wept. I told the story of El Salvador in my book, "Arthur, A Pilgrim" and shared how I trained him to preach and how sad I was at the death of my lovely parrot. These wonderful friends from Capetown and Durban had decided that they wanted to get me a parrot and Wendy had searched and searched all over South Africa until, amazingly, they found, perhaps the only Spanish speaking parrot in all of South Africa.

I was totally surprised as they presented me with a beautiful, large, green and multicolored parrot. "Como esta usted?" I cried. I put my hand against the cage and she got close. "Loreta, Loreta," she cried. That is her name. We fell in love at first sight. I spoke Spanish to her and she responded in love. She knew immediately that she was my sweetheart and we have had a glorious relationship ever since. The only problem is she doesn't want me to leave her and she doesn't want anyone but me! You can tell I'm madly in love with Loreta. One would never dream of receiving a parrot at such a time, but so is the mystery, surprise and excitement of life.

Last Morning of Fast

All morning, there was a constant flow of hundreds of people. They knew that I would be leaving today and many wanted to say good-bye. Others were desperate to be prayed for, pushing and shoving to get to the front. Others were waiting to receive Christ like a beautiful young model who spoke to me as she burst into tears, "I want to be born again." As noon approached, a huge crowd had gathered and I said, "Well praise the Lord, in all my time in South Africa there has not been one nasty thing said around the cross against us. It has absolutely been beautiful. I don't know of anywhere in the world that I've ever seen or felt more loved. You have loved me, I love you, I feel like South Africa is my home. If God would let me, I think I'd just take up residence here. I don't know of anywhere I'd rather live than in the park, in the middle of Durban. You've been my family and I've been your family. The call of God causes me to move on. God has made the world my home and I wish I could stay, but I am leaving today at noon and I go to Capetown and there will be fasting and praying in Capetown. The glory of God is in this place. The love of God. As all races are gathered around the cross, as all the people have come together in prayer and fellowship and nothing but beauty, it's just a shame that the whole world can't see how lovely it really is here. There are problems, but I tell you there are problems everywhere. Look at the way you all love one another and we're not going to let a few destroy the good of the many. The grace and the power and love of God is abundant. Now what I want us to do at twelve o'clock is to gather around the cross and bless this nation in the name of Jesus. The bible says what so ever you shall bind on earth shall be bound in heaven and loosed on earth shall be loosed in heaven and we're going to pray that the power of Satan will be bound from this nation. We know where hate comes from, it comes from the devil. We know where violence comes from, it comes from the devil, we know where injustice comes from, it comes from the devil. We want to pray for every family in South Africa to have a home, a job, justice, equality, a good education, good health and the blessings of God upon their lives. We want to thank God for the beautiful privilege we've had of gathering here day after day in liberty. I want us to bow down, we're going to pray and lay one hand on the ground, and one hand on somebody. We're going to claim the earth for the Lord and we're going to claim the people for the Lord and the blessings of God."

Dear heavenly Father, I pray Lord for Your blessings upon South Africa, we lay our hands upon this earth, the earth is the Lords, South Africa is the Lords, South Africa is not the devils. The devil can't have South Africa. Death can't have South Africa. Violence can't have South Africa. Jesus has come to save, bless and to pour out His Spirit upon this land. Dear God, as black and white and brown hands touch one another, we are one family, we are one nation, we have one Father God and we acknowledge You and ask You to bless us and prosper our land. Bless our families, give us jobs, health and happiness. In the name of Jesus may we have peace, love, justice, equality, purity in Jesus name, Hallelujah, Hallelujah, Praise You Lord, thank You Jesus. Let's say together the Lord's prayer right now. "Our Father, which art in heaven, hallowed by Thy name, Thy kingdom come, Thy will be done. On earth as it is in heaven. Give us this day our daily bread and forgive us our trespasses, as we forgive those who trespass against us and lead us not into temptation but deliver us from evil, for Thine is the kingdom and the power and the glory forever and ever." Amen. I just want to say this, thank you for loving me, thank you for loving the cross. Joshua and I are happy to have been with those of you who have been so kind. You will live in my heart forever. I leave my heart with you and I take your heart with me. Those of you that need to receive Jesus I want you to pray this prayer with me out loud. "Dear God, save my soul, forgive my sins in Jesus name, I repent, I welcome Jesus into my heart as Lord. I love You Lord and You are my Savior forever. I welcome You Jesus in my life and I welcome the Holy Spirit. Fill me with Your love, to love You God with all my heart, to love everyone, to love Your bible,and love Your church. Thanks for writing my name in heaven. I'm not ashamed of Jesus. In Jesus name, I pray. Amen" Now this is our final gathering and I think we ought to say a great thanks to the government officials who have been so happy to have us gather even during the state of emergency. I want us to do one thing symbolic before we finish. I want us to make one circle, put our arms around each other and have a circle around the cross. Would you do that, would you stand up? Isn't this beautiful, just look around, just look around you. This is South Africa. Hallelujah, praise the Lord! Look at the person standing beside you, whatever color they are, whatever language, this is the way God wants it to be. And this is the way it's going to be. "Our heavenly Father, we pray that You would make us one by Your grace. One family, one people, one nation under God in the name of Jesus Christ we ask You to bless these people and to bless this nation in the power of Your Holy Spirit this scene will live in our minds forever, in Jesus name we pray." Joshua and I love you. God bless you. Love each other. And I'll meet you in heaven. Glory to God.

This was a tremendous scene never to be forgotten. I had just received a copy of a letter written by the Chaplain of the U.S. Senate in Washington, D.C., Dr. Richard C. Halverson. In the letter he quotes George

MacLeod of Scotland:

> "I simply argue that the cross should be raised at the center of the marketplace as well as on the steeple of the church. I am recovering the claim that Jesus was not crucified in a cathedral between two candles, but on a cross between two thieves; on the town's garbage heap; at a crossroad, so cosmopolitan, they had to write His title in Hebrew and Latin and Greek...at the kind of a place where cynics talk smut, and thieves curse, and soldiers gamble. Because that is where He died. And that is what He died for. And that is what He died about. That is where church-men ought to be and what church-men ought to be about."

I laid down in the dirt with my face to the ground and prayed in silence. Then I stood, walked to the cross, knelt down beside it, made the sign of the cross over my chest, stood picking up my cross, Joshua grabbed his cross and we started to walk away. The crowds of people rushed to the cross and began crying, trying to touch us, wanting me to pray with them. It took perhaps fifteen minutes to make it out of the park. I felt joy and sadness. Durban was now behind us and Capetown was before me.

Capetown

Seven Days Fasting and Prayer
July 19 - 26, 1986

Capetown is without a doubt one of the most beautiful cities in the world with its high mountains, fabulous beaches, huge port, lovely office buildings, plush greenery of trees, flowers and grass. It also contains some of South Africa's neediest areas like the squatter camp at Crossroads.

The Lord burdened me to have the prayer and fast in front of the beautiful historic City Hall in an area called The Parade. Just behind City Hall is a beautiful view of the famous Table Mountain. Office buildings are on one side, the bus/train station is in front, the oldest military fort in South Africa is on the other side. This place had once been the beach where the first settlers arrived, the first preachers came and the first cross arrived. Now the cross had arrived again. We made our home on the steps of a large statue erected by the English years ago, a statue of Edward VII. I did not realize it at the time but at this statue most of the drunks, prostitutes, homosexuals, thieves and homeless travelers congregated. When Joshua and I arrived with the cross, the smell was almost unbearable. It reeked with the smell of urine and vomit and yet just a few feet away, there are famous flower stalls that are open until midnight every night. It was quite a place to make one's home.

The weather in Capetown in the wintertime is usually cold, rainy and windy, broken with short periods of sunshine. Joshua and I leaned our crosses against the statue and invited the group of Christians that were there to greet us to pray with us. Soon, crowds began to gather. Capetown is well known for its huge number of colored people, resulting from the whites of the past intermarrying with the local blacks. Now, I do not in any way like to keep using racial terms to identify people and I have sought in the book to keep those distinctions to a minimum. However, in South Africa, each person has been identified with a certain racial classification by the government as to whether they were white, colored, Indian or black. Even the housing regulations have been based upon these groupings. This is South Africa's largest area of coloreds. A beautiful crowd of people gathered as we were having prayer early this first night. All of a sudden, the lights went off. This entire area of the city was blacked out. The police said that a major switch had blown. I guess the holy surge of fire from heaven was too much. Ha!

In Capetown we also have another big clock that rings from City Hall every quarter hour. It was the same in Johannesburg and Durban. I can't believe it. Every fifteen minutes for twenty-one days and nights I have heard the chimes. It seems as though I could not live without the ringing of the bells.

In Capetown, because of the massive number of homeless people, (as this was shortly after the disastrous rioting and fighting in the black area of Crossroads and KCT where there were thousands of shacks burned down in a power struggle between various black factions and tribal groupings) to allow people to stay and sleep, we would have faced massive difficulties of logistics. So here, unlike Johannesburg and Durban, those who stayed the night all stayed awake praying and ministering as Joshua and I used our newly arrived Landrover camper which was parked only a few feet away as our place to sleep late at night.

Second Day

My heart is broken with so many of the street children who live day and night on the streets. We have been trying to help some. There are places that we can take everyone of the street children to live but the problem shockingly is that they could have a place to stay but they run away to live deliberately on these streets. That is the same problem with alcoholics and others that were here at night. We can take them to places where they can be cared for but the problem is in the heart which is typical of other big cities around the world. But we are seeing some converted and changed and we are placing them in various centers for help.

Once today, two men staggered up, sat down and leaned against the cross. I said, "Do you know what that is?" They looked. It was seven o'clock in the morning. They didn't even know that they had sat down against the cross. I explained the life of Jesus and invited them to Christ. Soon they both walked away. Then, one turned, rushed back to me and said, "I am sick of my life and I can't go on." He was converted. This morning one man took five new converts to his church.

I moved Loreta, my parrot, to my Landrover and now she is much happier to be near me. The sun is shining and I sit here for a quiet moment. The heat feels so good. The warmth of the sun speaks to the seeds and life springs forth. Sprouts grow and burst through the soil.

Soon green, then flowers, fruit and the cycle has been for ages. "Oh Lord, may Thy Son Jesus shine over South Africa warming the hearts, bringing forth the seeds of love bearing the fruit of peace, justice and blessings. Oh, I do love the warmth of the sun, the chilling coolness of the night, the smells and sounds of life. This is truly it. The cross in the crossroads of life. Life at its worst and its best. Lord help me to make it through, this has been a real mission."

As I was sitting here writing these words in my diary, the South African television came to film us again. They began to film me as I sat writing and then I saw this old man with only one eye who could barely walk with a slow shuffle. I could not stand to see him pass by. I got up, introduced myself to him and I read to him John 15:15 where Jesus said that He would be our Friend. I spoke to the man for a good while and then we prayed together. I saw a lovely girl who had been coming to pray and witness. She took the old man by his arm and helped him to sit down. She sat down with a friend of hers on the pavement in front of him and there this beautiful girl with blond hair, about twenty years old, sat talking to this old man who had no friend, who walked with a shuffle, who smelled like urine, and had one eye. This was a most beautiful sight. This is what life is about.

Later this afternoon, about 3:30, we were having prayer with a large group that had gathered. A lovely lady called for me to come to her as she stood at the edge of the crowd. When I got near her, she pulled me toward a man and a woman who were standing a short ways away. "Help me," she whispered. When I arrived at the couple, I noticed that the lady was wrestling to hold the man's hands down. She said, "Get the knife, get the knife," and then I saw this open knife with its flashing steel blade. I put my hand on the man's shoulder, slowly pushed the lady away and looked into the man's eyes. I said, "In the name of Jesus, hand me the knife." The man was weeping and trembling in rage. "I want revenge. I want to kill someone. My daughter was killed last Friday. I came here to kill someone but I saw the cross and I remember your son, a little boy, carrying his cross." He looked and saw Joshua. "There! That's the one, that's the boy. Oh God, forgive me, I need Jesus." He was shaking in hate. I put my hand on his hand and lifted the knife as his grip loosened. "Here, come with me to the cross." The crowd of people moved back as they saw this knife wielding man of revenge. Joshua and I prayed with him and he gave his life to Christ. He said, "I don't hate any more. I love everyone. If it hadn't been for the cross, I would have killed someone." The SABC television cameras had filmed this event. Some good Christian friends sat down with the man to do counseling and to help follow up.

One of the tragedies of human existence is the vicious desire for revenge and the inability of so many people to forgive. I have seen this over and over again. The evil act of one person justifies the evil act of another until that which is evil becomes normal and good and justifiable. As long as Northern Ireland lives in the memory of past injustices, there will be no peace today. As long as Lebanon seeks revenge for each cycle of killing, it is unending. If there are any two peoples that have suffered injustice throughout the years, it is the Jews and the Palestinians and yet because of unforgiveness and the spirit of revenge and payback, the bloody cycle continues. And so here, whether it be black tribal conflict or military conflict or discrimination and prejudice, until there is a time when one forgives no matter how great the atrocity, there can be no peace. The Christian cannot live with the injustices and the dishonor that was brought upon Christ 2,000 years ago by those responsible, nor can the Jews live without forgiveness concerning the atrocities of World War II, nor can the Indians of America live today upon the past injustices, nor can Americans live out today the atrocities and bitterness of our bloody civil war or the days of inhuman slavery in the South. This man's freedom from hatred and revenge at the cross offers hope for a troubled world today because at the cross we find reconciliation. For this is the universes greatest revelation. God offers peace and reconciliation, and the hope to the human race of coming into His family instead of pouring out revenge and destruction.

The television wanted me to go with the cross up to the top of Table Mountain which overlooks all of Capetown. The mountain is 3550 feet high and we had to ride to the top in a cable car. It was a beautiful view as the sun went down to a silvery sunset and we looked out over the city and prayed. How beautiful yet how great the need. These two thoughts filled my mind as we prayed through the night.

I will not attempt to give the daily events of my time in Capetown but simply to give a summary.

It was a glorious time of prayer and fasting and ministry. Some of the most beautiful Christians stayed with us in shifts day and night in very difficult weather conditions. The crowds were not as large as Johannesburg and Durban but the flow of people was constant with sometimes as many people gathered at three o'clock in the morning as in the day at noon. We had a very special ministry to the alcoholic and street people seeing many converted and leaving to become involved in churches and Bible studies. But one thing amazed me - I did not see one healing in Capetown and had only one person ask me to pray for them to be physically healed. I have no explanation. Even up to the last moment in Durban, people were being healed and hundreds of people were around begging for prayer and yet Capetown was like an entirely different country. The conviction of the Holy Spirit was just as great in Capetown but the manifestation of the glory of God was different.

I sit still
As the world vibrates around me
The cross stands in the city center
Some stare
Some pray
Some weep
Some smile
Some talk
The sounds of birds ---
Roaring traffic
And the chimes of the clock
On the quarter hour all make
Johannesburg, Durban and Capetown
        One
    Around the cross
Every color - language - condition
        One
The birds seem oblivious to
The problems the political leaders squabble about
I sit here contemplating it all
    (with God)

Just a day or so before the fast ended, I was sitting by the cross in the cold wind and rain. It was a beautiful time to pray as most people were not here in such weather. My mind was clear. The manifestation of the glory of God was so overwhelming. This was about the nineteenth or twentieth day that I'd been fasting and even though I had eaten a little between each seven day fast, I think the condition of my body and mind was equivalent to about twelve to fourteen days had I been fasting continuously. Let me say something about fasting.

Fasting over long periods of time is a spiritual experience. Now I didn't say that it was necessarily a Christian experience. It can and should be but the impact of fasting upon the mind and person is powerful, no matter who they may be. Almost all of the world's greatest spiritual and religious leaders have fasted for long periods of time. Moses fasted for forty days; Jesus fasted for forty days; other religious leaders have traditionally fasted. When one fasts, it is imperative that they constantly be in the Word of God, the Bible, lest they be deceived by evil spirits and possessed with evil, even in the cloak of goodness. I fasted once in Hollywood, California for twenty-eight days with just water in my struggle to maintain our street ministry in Hollywood. I fasted in Washington, D.C. along with my wife, Sherry, for forty days as we prayed for our nation and the cleansing of it in Washington. My wife was pregnant with Joshua who is now by my side, and ate nothing during much of the third and fourth months of her pregnancy. My wife and I also fasted in Northern Ireland in the middle of the troubles there for three days and nights. After about ten to twelve days of fasting, the mind and body become incredibly clear. I can think on any subject as long as I want to without my mind drifting. Concentration is incredible. After approximately one to three days, all hunger pains are gone because the stomach has formed a chemical coating to protect it from the acids that would normally be used to digest food. As this book is not a theological text book, I shall not try to give all Bible references to fasting, except to say that fasting was a normal Biblical principle that often happened. Any good Bible concordance will list all references to fasting. Fasting helps purify the body and the mind. A partial list of some who fasted is:

        Moses - Exodus 34:27 & 28
        The Israelites - Leviticus 16:29
                        I Samuel 7:5 & 6
        David - II Samuel 1:11 & 12
        Elijah - I Kings 19:2 & 8
        Nehemiah - Nehemiah 1:4
        Daniel - Daniel 9:3 & 4
                        Daniel 10:2 & 3
        Anna - Luke 2:36 & 37
        The disciples of Jesus and John - Matthew 9:14
        Jesus - Matthew 4:1 & 2
        Paul - Acts 14:23
        Cornelius - Acts 10:30

        Jesus said in Matthew 17:21 "This kind cometh not out but by prayer and fasting." Throughout the Bible, there are numerous declarations of where people repented and fasted or fasted and were cleansed and empowered. This twenty-one days of fasting and prayer for me was in obedience to the direct call of God. I did it in obedience. I do not try to analyze it. I simply have tried to live it. I know God has heard our prayers and not just the prayers of those who have gathered around this physical cross but others by the millions in South

Africa that are praying in their churches, homes and prayer groups; through television programs in the West such as Trinity Broadcasting and CBN, Kenneth Copeland, Richard Roberts, and numerous others. Tens of millions of people have been mobilized to pray for South Africa at this time.

As I sat in the cold rain contemplating the things of God, I suddenly said to the Lord, "Oh God, show me something profound, something deeper than I've ever thought about before, something I need, something that is the ultimate in understanding and revelation that I have been blinded to." The words from John, the fourth chapter, verses twenty-three and twenty-four came to my mind: "But the hour cometh, and now is, when the true worshipers shall worship the Father in spirit and in truth: for the Father seeketh such to worship Him. God is a Spirit; and they that worship Him must worship Him in spirit and in truth." These words staggered me. I had never really dwelt on them, even though I had preached so many sermons from this very chapter. I was now thinking differently than I had ever thought about this particular passage before. What does it mean - worship in spirit and in truth? Jesus said that from then on, that's how we were to worship and yet I had never really studied what that meant. Then I began to see an unfolding picture in my mind. Jesus said God is a Spirit. God is Spirit. What does that mean? What is Spirit? Spirit is presence, not a term, it is the presence of God. God said to Moses in Exodus 33:14, "My presence shall go with thee." Jesus said we must worship the Father in spirit and in truth. This means that where God's Spirit is, His presence is. Where God's presence is, His Spirit is and where His Spirit is, His presence is. I have presence. I occupy space where my body is. That is my physical presence. If someone is sitting near me talking to me they would say, "I am in the presence of Arthur Blessitt." I have a presence but God also has a presence. It is where His Spirit is. So true worship then is when we are in His presence with our presence. Jesus said, "If you have seen Me, you have seen the Father." We are to worship in His presence. He is here to those who are born into his kingdom we are with Him. His presence is deep, personal, imminent and always available to the believer. Wherever I am, God is. You can come into my presence but you can come into God's presence and live in His presence. As we worship Him in spirit, we recognize His presence. Jesus was speaking to the Samaritan woman as the story is described in John the fourth chapter. They had their special mountain where they felt that God was. As she said in verse twenty, "Our fathers worshiped in this mountain and You say that in Jerusalem is the place where men ought to worship." For this woman and most of the people of her day, the concept was that God's presence inhabited a certain geographical place. Jesus was now saying no, not in that mountain, nor in Jerusalem shall we worship the Father but from now on, the true worshipers shall worship the Father in spirit and in truth. Jesus was saying now you can worship Him anywhere. He will be with us, not a geographical location, but His Spirit, His presence, will be wherever you are. When God is present, all God is, is present. There is no part of God, only God. He is all the time. It is we who are such narrow funnels that little manifestation of His presence and Spirit is revealed. The problem is not that God in all His glory and works is not present, but that we limit the manifestation of His presence. God is a Spirit. We must be present in His presence. This is truly worship. Again the Bible says He inhabits the praises of His people (Psalm 22:3). His presence is within our praises while we are within His presence. He is in us while we are in Him. The extent of the revelation of His glorious presence is available only to them that are available and capable of receiving it. The depth of which we may know the intimate heart of God is also based upon our capacity and sensitivity to receive it.

God had me contemplate upon the Spirit throughout the afternoon and early night. Then I moved on to the next word - TRUTH. Jesus said we must worship the Father in spirit and in truth. What does that word truth mean? In essence, truth means total honesty. Truth is absolute revealing. Truth means nothing concealed or covered - naked like Adam and Eve. The first man God ever spoke to was unclothed. The first woman God ever spoke to was unclothed. The first couple God ever spoke to was unclothed. God walked with them in the Garden. He talked with them. They were together naked in the presence of God. This was true worship and this is what we are to be, Jesus said. But something happened. When Adam and Eve sinned against God, being deceived by Satan, the first thing that happened was they knew that they were naked and they made a covering of fig leaves. Then they hid from the presence of God. The Lord came walking in the Garden and called unto Adam. "Where art thou?" Adam said, "I was afraid because I was naked and I hid myself." And God said, "Who told you that you were naked?" Adam and Eve had never seen any clothes. They had never heard of clothes. And God said who told you you were naked? It was Satan; and people have from that time until this, been trying to cover up and hide from God. Notice how this woman told the truth, yet lied. In verse fifteen, the woman said to Jesus: "Give me this water that I thirst not neither come here to draw" as Jesus had told her that He had living water. Now she wanted what Jesus had to offer but in order to receive it, she had to come in truth. Therefore, Jesus said to her, "Go call your husband and come here." The woman answered and said, "I have no husband." Jesus said, "You have well said 'I have no husband' (You told the truth). For you have had five husbands and he whom you now have is not your husband. In that you told the truth." Now here, you see the typical manifestation of telling the truth and lying at the same time. Technically, she told the truth. 'I have no husband,' but basically, Christ was revealing to her that He wanted openness and truth - real truth - not technical truth because in essence she had lied. She had had five husbands and was now living with a man though not technically her husband. She got the point immediately because she said, "I perceive that You are a prophet," because now she was dealing with Someone who knew her, not just heard her words. That is what truth is. Truth is open, exposed, with no covering of our will, mind, or motive. If I were to call my wife on the telephone from here and ask her how she is, she could say, "Fine" and I would believe her and accept that she told the truth. But she could have had an accident and broken her legs and be in a cast in great pain, but since I am not in her presence, I only have her words and in a technical sense, she might be fine, but not truly fine in the greater meaning of the word. If I were present with her, she could not conceal that condition. That is how we are to worship in spirit and in truth. We worship in His presence (Spirit), uncovered and unashamed (truth). Jesus was showing her that God's presence was not in that mountain or in Jerusalem but that the temple of God's presence shall be within you. The holy of holies of God's presence will be your heart. (I Corinthians 6:19-20). This woman did recognize the presence of God and did comprehend the truth of her condition, Jesus revealed something to the woman that He did not even say to the disciples when she asked about the Messiah. Jesus said, "I that speak to you am He."

After the resurrection of Jesus, as two of the disciples were on the road to the village of Emmaus, Jesus also joined them along the road and they spoke to Him. He taught them all the things from Moses through the prophets concerning the Christ. Finally, when they arrived at the house in the evening, Jesus sat down and joined them for the meal. Jesus took the bread and blessed it and gave it to them, their eyes were opened and they knew Him. Jesus had been with them along the road that day but they had not worshiped Him. Their hearts were sad because they thought He was still in the tomb. True worship is the recognition of His presence in our presence and the understanding that He knows us and we are open and free and uncovered with Him. The amazing concluding work is this that Jesus said, "The Father seeketh such to worship Him." God is looking for those who will worship in His presence, in His spirit and truth with nothing hidden. If we reveal ourselves, He will reveal Himself.

On the final Saturday morning, just before we concluded the fast, a policeman who was on duty in our general area came up and made this comment to me: "When you walk all around this area, it's normal, but when people go there (pointing towards the steps of the statue where the cross stood), then you mean business." Late one evening, an old drunk man staggered up as we were sitting in quiet prayer. He hollered out very loudly, "Why are you fools gathered around Edward the VII?" as he gazed up at the statue. "Why, he's been dead long ago." One of the men got up and began sharing Christ with him. I sat there rejoicing. Praise God, we're serving a living and resurrected Christ. He's alive in this world today. We know Him and yet for so many around, they are blinded to His presence and power. Hallelujah, He's alive!

As a great crowd gathered to close out the twenty-one days of fasting and prayer, we had another great footwashing service but this time in the open air around the cross. Again, it was people of all races. It was glorious beyond words. I closed by reading these words from the book of Numbers chapter six, verses twenty-three through twenty-six: "As the Lord spoke to Moses saying, Like this you shall bless the children of Israel (South Africa), say unto them: The Lord bless you and keep you. The Lord make His face to shine upon you and be gracious unto you. The Lord lift up His countenance upon you and give you peace."

The Walk With the Cross
in South Africa

From late October 1985 through January 1986, I was walking with the cross in Southern Africa. I returned again in 1986 from the 1st of June through August. Part of that time, I was fasting and praying with the cross in the city centers. The rest of the time, I was carrying the cross. Most of the time, I was walking in the Republic of South Africa and in what is called independent countries, sometimes known as homeland states like Ciskei, Venda, etc. Yet their independence is recognized only by South Africa and not the rest of the world. Other countries like Lesotho and Botswana are recognized internationally though I only walked in those two countries very briefly. I will share with you some of the highlights of this walk and also some typical days along the road that will give you the flavor of my life and the response in South Africa.

My arrival in South Africa began, strangely enough, not with the sound of gravel against my feet as I carried the cross, but with the thud of airplane wheels against the runway and the reverse thrust of the jet engines of a private lear jet as Paul Crouch and I arrived in South Africa in September 1984. Paul, along with his lovely wife, Jan, are two of my closest companions. They are the founders and president of Trinity Broadcasting Network in Southern California, who by the leadership of our Lord, have established the worlds largest full time twenty-four hour a day, Christian television network. Paul and I, with his son

Matthew, met with the President of Ciskei. He graciously welcomed us to build a Christian television station in their country which viewing audiences will include a section of the Republic of South Africa and the large city of East London. A year later, in September 1985, Paul and I arrived again in Ciskei. On the way we had met with the Presidents of Kenya and Zaire. I preached to the Ciskei government cabinet and also was out in some villages filming my daily television program that is shown on TBN. The people in the villages were so warm and friendly and they were eager for me to come to them with the cross. My heart was being gripped by God for South Africa. Much of the TV station was built, including the tower. Mr. Douw Steyn, Special Assistant to the President of Ciskei, was always so helpful and kind to us.

We left for America with a refueling stop in Windhoek, South West Africa, even though we were only there at the airport for a couple of hours, I knew one day I would return and walk there.

I arrived back in Los Angeles on September 21. On Monday, September 23, Paul called me on the telephone and said, "Arthur, come down to the Anaheim Convention Center and help me give a brief report on Africa before we air the Kenneth Copeland crusade on TV. You can also give an invitation for people to receive Christ at the end of the meeting." I had never met Kenneth Copeland personally. Sherry and I, along with Paul and Jan, opened the television program and after about forty-five minutes, we switched live inside the huge auditorium to their program in progress.

I met Kenneth Copeland during the opening minutes of the program. We were seated in an out-of-the-way place near the platform. Suddenly Kenneth Copeland turned to me and said these burning words:

"Arthur Blessitt, I gotta tell you something from the Lord. Your humility and integrity has come up before God and is to be admired even by other men because you walked in hard spots, did what I told you to do when it was impossible. I've been trying to tell you for days now how much I appreciate you and every time I start talking to you to tell you how much I appreciate you, you start running backwards and telling me that you don't deserve that. I wish you'd quit that. I want you to know this, I esteem you highly, I walk with you as a son, not just a child. My spirit has been opening the door for you to come walk in boldly and I admire the humility of your heart."

I said, "I've been in many wars in the last 16 years and sitting here I knew, the Lord said to me I want you to carry the cross into South Africa and to leave within the next 30 days. And I will go to South Africa to walk to the middle of those riots and battlefields with the good news of Jesus Christ and His love. And I need you to pray for me. I've been gone 3 months and I've just been home 2 days. It's tough to leave again."

Then he responded, "The Lord wanted me to tell you that He understands that you haven't been home very long, but if there was anybody else for the job He'd send them, but you have to go do it son. God's going to fill your steps with joy, fill your hands with this healing power and anoint you more than you've ever been anointed in your life. You are going to see the glory of God before you get home. Hallelujah."

He received the nightly offering without saying how it would be used. Afterward he announced that it would be given to our cross walking witness and that his ministry would match the amount given. God had blessed me, called me and provided the support for our South African trip, all in an unusual way.

* * *

Joshua and I were looking at a map of South Africa. We were in the camping van that Mr. Richard Scallan had arranged for us to use. As we prayed, suddenly one place leaped out at us - Port Edward. We knew no one there but it was located along the coast, south of Durban. The Lord said, "That's where you are to begin and you will get your driver at Margate." It is a large holiday town north of Port Edward. With great joy, we headed toward that place to begin our walk with the cross.

The next day, we arrived in Margate and stayed in a hotel. When I woke up, the Lord said, "Go walk around the block. Turn left at the hotel, go down to the corner, down one block, around to the right and back to the hotel. I'll lead you to the driver." I told Joshua I would be back with the driver and I left. As I walked around the block, I spoke to probably ten different people on the sidewalk or in shops. Everyone said, go to the Unemployment Agency on the main highway. I began to walk slowly as I was now only a few feet from the hotel. What I'm going to tell you is the total truth. At the last parking place before the hotel entrance a white pickup truck pulled in front of me and stopped. As he opened the door, I told him that I was looking for a driver to drive my camping van. I explained nothing else. He looked up and said to me, "My construction work is a little slow at this time. I have a driver free."

His name was Mr. John Williams. After a short conversation, he said, "If you'd like, we can drive out now and make all the arrangements, but first could we stop by a house that we are remodeling?" I said, sure. When we arrived at the house, he said, "You're welcome to come in. It's very hot in the truck." The house was located in Southbroom which is perhaps the most prestigious resort center in South Africa with homes built around a golf course by the seaside. Inside the house, I met a young man in his mid twenties named Mark Bernett. We sat down and began to talk. He asked me what I was doing and I said I needed a driver to drive my van and Mr. Williams was taking me to arrange it. Mark said, "I'll be your driver." But I couldn't afford to hire someone like you," I said, looking about at the luxurious home. He said, "Oh, I'll do it for free or for anything you want to give." I said, "But there's another thing." I explained to him that I was walking, carrying a big cross and that Joshua was walking also with the cross and every other day, Joshua would be doing his correspondence school work in the van. We had thousands of pieces of gospel material that we would use the van to carry for us to give out to the people. I asked him if he knew Jesus as his Savior. He said, "No. I'm just your normal sinner but I think I may be an alcoholic." He was such a lovely man and I heard God whisper to me, "Take him, this is your driver." Mark can speak the local African language of this area, Zulu, very well and he told me this story: "Last week, I was sitting in London in a pub drinking. My life was totally messed up. Then for the first time in my life, something spoke to me 'go back to South Africa and get involved with driving American visitors around. Go now." He said, "I knew that the tourist business in South Africa was in disastrous shape, yet I knew I had to go." He flew to Johannesburg then drove down here and now I arrived. The

Lord had brought me from America, to Johannesburg, to Margate, to a walk around the block, to a house being remodeled, and had brought my driver, and soon-to-be buddy, from a pub in London to Johannesburg, to the beach house.

Mark did not receive Christ that day, but the next morning, he arrived at my hotel early. He was an awful mess. He had been drinking all night. He had a terrible headache and was sick, yet I knew he was to be my driver. Joshua and I unloaded our crosses at Port Edward and before we began the walk, we put our arms around Mark and we knelt along the roadside and we prayed. I didn't know it at the time, but it was his first public prayer meeting and it almost scared him to death. That day, as crowds gathered, Mark served as my Zulu interpreter. Late in the afternoon, Mark and I prayed together and he received Jesus as his Savior and was born again. He said, "I am a new man," and sure enough, he was!

Two weeks later, we baptized him in the Indian Ocean and he traveled with me for two months and is now doing a lot of witnessing as he runs his father's insurance company in Johannesburg.

South Coast

I tell you, it has been glorious. All along this highway, car after car stopped. Blacks, Indians, whites, poor ladies working along the roadsides and ladies in Mercedes Benz, but the awesome thing is that all people are waving, smiling. Glory to God! A young lady in her boutique shop had just received the newspaper. She had it laying on the counter in front of her and was reading the front page about the cross. She whispered, "God, I can't find You. If only I could meet this man." She looked up and there in the rain in front of her shop was Joshua and I. She called out to us. We went to her and she gloriously received Christ.

Another day I write, "Well, glory to God. It's great and glorious. The walk has turned into a slow crawl. People stopping, cars stopping everywhere. Sometimes there was literally no place for another car to park. The roadside was jammed. People so hungry for Jesus, eager for God - of all races - no problem at all except how to deal with so many beautiful and eager people."

Johannesburg

Joshua and I flew to Johannesburg to preach at the huge Rhema Church. We arrived for the Sunday morning service late expecting that I would only attend the morning meeting because I was scheduled to preach the night service. When the pastor saw me, he said, "God has told me not to preach. We'll sing one more song, then you preach." I was shocked but of course, ready, and God gave me a powerful message from Revelation, the first chapter, where John said, "I was in the spirit on the Lord's day." It was a glorious meeting. At night I preached on the words of Jesus, "I will be with you always." I took off my shoes during the sermon and showed the people my feet where by the grace of God, there are no marks, no scars and even no calluses. And they were amazed and so am I at the constant miracle of God in my feet. In Romans 10:15, it says, "How beautiful are the feet of them that preach the gospel of peace and bring glad tidings of good things." The church is such a blessing. They run over 5,000 people a meeting. It is completely multiracial. How blind the world is to the beauty of such multiracial gospel churches as this in South Africa.

Durban

When I arrived in Durban, I preached at the Durban Christian Center which meets in an old theater in the center of town. Here again, is a huge multiracial church of thousands with associated mission churches all over South Africa, all multiracial and moving in the power of the Holy Spirit under the direction of a beautiful, powerful man of God, Reverend Fred Roberts. When I started out of downtown Durban toward the beach, we spent all day and only made three kilometers (about two miles) because person after person was stopping us on the streets. Crowds were gathering. The response was great, powerful and it is almost completely impossible to walk because of the eagerness and hunger of the people.

Chesterfield

It was a great day today! As I went through this black area, people rushed from their homes, children poured into the streets and we saw the beautiful love of the people as they welcomed the cross and the message of Jesus and the joy, life, peace, hope and salvation that He gives.

Phoenix

Today, I ate in the home of an old Hindu Indian man. He was excited beyond words to see the cross and compelled me to come into his house. He took me in to his bedroom where there was a picture of Jesus hanging on the wall, and he told me this story. He said just a few days before he'd had a vision. He saw the cross rising up from the ground and he was coming to it. He heard a great crowd of people singing and praising God behind him and he came with a great garland of flowers to put them on the cross. Then he heard a voice from behind the cross that said, "Soon the Big Father will come to you, soon you will know the Big Father." Today the cross did come to him and we prayed together and he welcomed Jesus into his heart and now he knows "the Big Father."

Tongaat

This area is very much like what I was in earlier this year in India. The population is predominantly Indian all along this coast north of Durban. The people welcomed me in the deepest way possible. There is great understanding of a man walking on foot with the cross. Tonight I left my cross inside a supermarket and ate in the home of the Kader family, who run the Shell gas station. Almost all the people in this area are Hindus or Moslems.

Tongaat Next Day

Tonight I stayed with the lovely Naicker family who have a Mobile gas station and market. She gave the most beautiful meal you could ever eat and treated us so kindly. We had wonderful Bible study about Jesus and I prayed together with her entire family. They put "Jesus stickers" all over the station and market and welcomed me and Joshua and the cross with open arms.

Amatikulu

What a glorious day it has been along the road with

the cross! All the people are so lovely and the response continues to be overwhelming. I know that it's difficult for people to comprehend this because most people think that South Africa is exploding in a blood bath every day. They have no idea how much understanding and love and what beautiful people they are of all races that live here.

Last night just before dark, I arrived in a village, the crowd of people led us to a small house where there was a man filled with demon spirits who fell on the floor and began to froth at the mouth and scream. I prayed over him along with Joshua. The demons were cast out and he was set free. This morning, he was in his right mind. And today along the roads, it has been so hot, oh, so hot! About mid afternoon, the owner of a sugar cane plantation stopped and said, "My house is just there and I have a swimming pool. You are welcome to spend the night with us tonight, have a good swim and a meal. It was absolutely fantastic as we splashed and swam and laughed, Joshua and Mark and I. We thought for a moment that we were on holiday. Ha! and in some ways, I guess we were - everyday with Jesus is sweeter than the day before!

Eshowe

Well today was unbelievable. It was so good! People, people, people. Car after car, truck after truck. I'm now in the Zulu area of South Africa. It's the historic homeland of the Zulus. It is the largest tribal group by far in South Africa with over eight million Zulus. They are the most unbelievable people in their welcome of the cross. I do not exaggerate by saying you could look to your right and see crowds coming toward the cross; you could look to your left and see crowds coming to the cross; look straight ahead and see crowds coming to the cross. When I arrived in this town which I think is one of the most lovely small towns in its physical beauty and one of the greatest towns in their hearts to welcome the cross, crowds of people swarmed around the cross. They came from everywhere and emptied store after store. One owner of a clothing store even invited me inside the store to preach. I preached in the street over and over and we gave out thousands and thousands of pieces of gospel material. Tonight, I also preached at the Rotary Club to the businessmen of the city. It's a day I can never forget in this beautiful mountainous area seeing all the people running to the cross and crowds of blacks and whites gathered together as one family.

Melmoth

Well, today was indescribable. I preached eighteen sermons as well as walked. I began with the cross at 4:45 in the morning. Can you believe it - in these mountains, and yet it was so hot and at every hill or valley, there was a group of people rushing to the cross.

It was fabulous. South African television came and filmed a program in Zulu and English. I will never forget at one mountain pass, there were about fifty Zulu ladies selling fruit just off the road. As I arrived with the cross, they began to clap and sing and dance. They were singing a Zulu gospel song. They forgot about their marketing and they all gathered around me bursting forth in joy and praise as I had climbed up that mountain. I talked with them as one lady interpreted and they gave me a huge bag of fruit. The fruit seemed to be heavier than the cross and I couldn't wait to catch up with the van to put the fruit in! But those people so full of joy, I just wish I'd had a camera to record it. These people feel so deep, they can't believe that I've come so far bringing the cross to them. And they are all excited that I'm going to see the chief of the Zulus in Ulundi very soon. Often the cross is completely stopped. It is impossible to walk. When I got into Melmoth, there was complete and total chaos and I'm not stretching this at all. All the children left the school and were gathered by the highway. Because my walk was so slow the entire morning there were no classes while the students waited for the cross to arrive. In the middle of the town again, all the stores were emptied and near the bus station thousands of people were welcoming the cross. Big black men weeping, white women crying, people smiling full of joy, bursting into singing. I cannot imagine any response greater than this.

Ulundi

As I made my way along the road to Ulundi, there was total chaos. Everyone knew that I was on the way to meet Chief Minister Buthelezi. I carried the cross to the Legislative Assembly as this is the capital of Kwazulu. Chief Minister Mangosuthu Buthelezi came out personally to escort Joshua and me into the Assembly. In the Assembly that day there were gathered approximately one hundred of the top leaders of Iinkarta which are the ruling leaders of the Zulu people. Chief Buthelezi said, "We have had many people come to visit us. They come by plane, they come by car, but this is the first man to walk to us and he brings with him the symbol of our hope and salvation, the cross. We welcome him with all our hearts." As I stood there looking at these men and women my heart was filled with deep emotion. Before I could speak tears burst from my eyes and the people too began to weep. I shared with them the good news of our Lord Jesus Christ, the dream of the angels - peace on earth, goodwill toward men and pointed out that in Christ there is unity, justice, equality. There is no discrimination. I commended them for their stand of peace and love. I read to them Scripture from the words of Jesus, shared how God had burdened me to come with the cross and walk through South Africa praying for peace and reconciliation. Finally, on one of the few occasions of my life, I knew that I had to do this special thing. I got down on my hands and knees beside the cross, took my knife and cut two small pieces from the cross and I gave it to Chief Buthelezi for his courageous stand against violence and for his desire for there to be change and reconciliation without bloodshed. He said that this was the greatest gift that he had ever received. I then knelt to pray for him and the people. Suddenly I noticed the entire Assembly had knelt together and we had one of the most glorious prayer meetings I had ever been in. Afterwards, Chief Buthelezi invited me to have dinner with him at the Holiday Inn. Joshua and I, Mark Bernett, Chief Buthelezi and his sister Ruth Makiwani and Reverend Dr. Alphaeus Zulu shared a meal and our hearts with each other. Chief Buthelezi is head of the largest grouping of people in South Africa; much larger than the white population of approximately three and a half million and represents approximately one-third of the entire black population. Iinkarta is the largest organization in South Africa with over one million dues-paying members. Chief Buthelezi said these words to me:

> "If I didn't have Christ as the rudder to give
> me direction when things are difficult I
> wouldn't have survived up to now. In this
> country, we have many leadership roles,
> nations and race groups that are in conflict.

My commitment to Christ teaches me that all the people of this country, white or black, are all God's children. Our conflicts are not unique, they have happened in many countries and nations. I therefore believe, as a follower of Christ, Christ loves me as much as He loves the state president, Mr. Botha. I would say politically we are in conflict. I realize that he is a brother because he believes in Christ. I am not happy about the way he rules me and my people. Without Christ I would have thrown my hands up in desperation and quit. I think that the Christians in America can help by praying for us. The problems of this country can be resolved peacefully. The problems of this country must not be resolved by bloodshed but by peaceful means. We are challenged by the law, Christ said was above all laws; by loving our neighbor as ourselves."

I laid hands on him and prayed over him for the blessings of God, the wisdom of God, and his safety. We shared together our deep companionship in the pathway of Jesus Christ.

On The Road - Somewhere

Today I preached fifteen times. I am getting nearer to Johannesburg now, closer there than back to Durban. It was very hot climbing on mountain roads all day, then it began to rain. I saw this big black cloud and I knew it was going to pour rain. Just as the cloud burst, I looked for somewhere to get shelter, and there was a small village of only a few houses. They were mud huts made round with a thatch straw roof. As I approached the first house, I saw two men sitting inside and I asked if I could come in. They said, "Yes." One of the men could speak English and I sat down on a large empty can and joined them around the fire. The man asked me what I was doing with that big cross and I shared with him. Then he said, "I know why you've come. I know why the rain came, so that you would come to my house. Next door is my home and my wife is very sick. She is about to die and there is no help for her. Please come with me and pray for her." I went into the house, laid hands on the lady and she was immediately healed, stood up and joined us with her two children. Because of the outpour of rain, Joshua and Mark came driving back in the van to find me. They saw the cross outside the house and came in. There was a time of great rejoicing as the lady was healed and then as they all received Christ. He said, "I know now God likes us because in the Bible when Jesus came into town, He saw one man who was a great sinner, in a tree. He called down Zacchaeus and said, 'I'm coming to your house.' God has sent you just like that to us today." We were all weeping and felt such a bond of love.

My shoes had completely worn through at the soles and the day before I had bought a new pair of shoes to protect my feet from the rough, rocky roadsides. I gave this new pair of shoes to this poor man with great joy for it is more blessed to give than to receive. I knew in all his life he would never be able to afford such a pair. He was happy beyond words. I don't like to say much about it but I bring with me, whenever possible, thousands of dollars to give to needy people and to special ministries, pastors and to help the poor. Day after day, I have the privilege of doing this as people have shared their generosity with me, I pass it on. Joshua and I went to the van and we got food and clothes and supplies to leave with that family. I only wish that

I had enough to give to everyone. Somehow I think that it must be easy for the affluent western woman or man with all their needs supplied, to want to bring economic suffering upon the South of Africa; but they have no idea what suffering really is. To be poor and discriminated against is a tragedy. To afflict the poor even more is heartbreaking beyond words.

Soweto - Johannesburg

After arriving with the cross in Johannesburg just before Christmas, Joshua and I felt so excited. We had done a long walk of almost a thousand kilometers now and yet the mission with the cross walk was not over. I knew there was one place that I must go - Soweto. Day after day along the road from Durban toward Johannesburg, cars and trucks and buses had stopped and so many had said, "When you get to Johannesburg, you must come and visit us in Soweto." This is the largest black township in South Africa known the world over for their riots, boycotts and problems with the police and military. Joshua had felt he should be home before Christmas and so as he left to go back to his mother, brothers and sisters. I prepared in my heart to go to Soweto and then on to Namibia, South West Africa. I walked into Soweto on Sunday morning, December 22nd. It was a day I will never forget. So many people feared for my life. There was a state of emergency in that area and Soweto was under marshal law. All public meetings and news media were banned. As I walked over the hill, I could see Soweto lying in front of me in this great valley plain. It is difficult to describe what happened, but I knelt looking at the city and then lay down upon the ground and prayed. The glory of God covered me. I walked in alone except for God and His holy angels. I had a large bag filled with gospel materials and thousands of Jesus stickers tied to the cross. As I approached the first houses, people began to respond by coming to the cross. Many of the people had seen the cross on television as we had been in the news and also in the newspapers. It was Sunday, so men, women and children were home. It was just a "Jesus day." Over and over again, it was a constant flow of people as I walked down the main road through the heart of Soweto and then off to one side, and then another; blocks out of the way as people would invite me to their house to have something to eat or drink. This happened in home after home with the whole yard and street filled with people. Many of the people could not believe that a white man would walk through the center of Soweto but they were happy that I had come. I don't believe that I've ever, in seventeen years, eaten more food and drank more drinks in one day, than this day. This had do be the world record! Even though there are needs in Soweto and great tragedies have happened there, I found a reservoir of love that is indescribable. This area is not a squatter's camp like Crossroads which is basically a settlement without sewage or normal services as it is technically an illegal settlement. But Soweto is different with very neat, clean though modest homes with sewage, running water, electricity and most homes with televisions, radios - very different from what I had imagined it would be. I did not receive one word of anger or hatred - only welcome. I'll never forget this one scene and even though it was forbidden to take pictures, I had brought my camera along to record the fact of my walk through this area. I have a photograph of the following scene. As I walked into an area where most of the mini buses, taxis, and large buses are concentrated, crowds of people were all around me as I preached and shared the good news of Christ and the message of the cross. As I preached and prayed with people, I noticed that I was surrounded, almost entirely, by men who were the drivers of all these buses and vans which carried the people into the cities and to their jobs. As I was finishing and speaking to the men who were crowded around me, I noticed that someone was collecting money and that the people were putting money into a hat. Finally, the man approached me with this money made up of small coins. He said, "We want to give you this money to help you on your way with the cross." I said, "I don't accept money from the churches along the way where I am walking, nor from individuals. I've come to give, not to receive and certainly I couldn't take money from you in Soweto because the needs here are so great and I know the needs of you and your families. Tears were pouring down my cheeks. I had never seen a greater gesture than these poor men wanting to help me. And yet they interrupted me, all of them shaking their heads, "No, you must accept it." They began to speak. I'll never forget what they were saying. "You brought the cross to us. You brought hope which is more than anything. You brought us the cross; you came yourself to be with us in our suffering. Our situation is so difficult and seems impossible but we can see and feel that you understand. We are poor men and we have suffered under the apartheid system, under discrimination that we've received in the past. And yet, we suffer also from the hands of some of our own people. We have children and families and we must work to feed them but the youth gangs - they have no work and no families. They try to keep everyone from working. They try to burn our buses and vans and taxis. They've tried to burn us. They drag women from our buses and pour out their groceries because they bought them in town. These gangs try to burn our houses because we work and they want us not to work, but if we don't work, we will all starve to death, so we must work. But every day we face discrimination from one part of society and we face violence and death from another part of society. It seems hopeless for us. What can we do? The only hope is what you speak about the love of Jesus, the white and black can love each other and that black will learn to love black and that we will try to help each other. We have no voice, we have no vote. The government does not seem to want to hear us and the youth gangs do not want to hear us. Will you speak for us and tell the world we only want peace and justice? Please, you must take this money. It is the only thing that expresses what we feel in our hearts." Those black men began to hug me and cry. How could I refuse? I raised my hands and said, "I want us all to get on our knees and pray again." We knelt together and I prayed, crying, as I asked God to bless them and give them peace, protection, justice, that discrimination and violence would be gone. I stood and looked at them, I knew their love, I could feel the injustice that they felt and I could comprehend their fear because there was a huge boycott on at that very moment and anyone who was working or shopping in Johannesburg did so under the threat of death because if any were found to have merchandise that they had bought in the city, they'd have broken the boycott. These men and hundreds of thousands like them were in a desperate situation. I said I would take their money and would give most of it to other people that I met that were in need in Soweto. And yet as I put some of the small coins in my pocket by my heart, I said, "I will take this money with me and I will keep it as long as I live and I will carry you in my heart forever and I will never forget you." I picked up the cross and walked on and they walked back to their buses and vans and every time since when I read that another bus has been burned or the driver burned to death or hacked to death, I wonder if it's one of the men that I prayed with. Shortly after this, a group of young men were around me and I was explaining to them what I was doing. One of the guys said, "Would you come with us to our house and have something to drink?" I could tell that these young men were very rowdy and possibly very dangerous, yet this is what it's all about. These are the kind of people I need to talk with. I said, "Yes." And I went with them. They came to a small house several blocks away and the house soon filled with young men - no children, no women, only young men. One man said, "Don't you feel danger? Aren't you afraid?" I said, "No, I feel that I'm among friends. I come in peace with the love of God. What do you guys do?" They looked at each other and began to laugh. "Well, we rob, we burn, we kill." I said, "Then would you say that you're the toughest group in Soweto?" With seeming pride, they said, "Yes." Again they laughed, and so did I. I said, "So if you guys are my friends, I guess there's nothing I have to worry about." They looked at each other, they looked back at me and I said, "Jesus loves you, so do I." As I began to speak to the entire group the message of Christ, they interrupted me saying, "Oh, our mothers go to church." I said, "What about you?" They said, "No, we don't." But one of the men spoke up and said, "Would you pray for us?" I looked them all in the eye and said, "No, but I will pray with you. There's a lot of difference." I dropped to my knees beside the couch, looked up at them and said, "kneel down and I'll pray with you." They began to look at each other. Finally, one bowed and then another, until the entire house of young men were on their knees and I said, "Let me teach you a prayer." And as I began to lead them in the Lord's prayer, I noticed many of them already knew the words. And then I led in a prayer of commitment to Christ. Only God knows who did and did not mean it in their heart. I stood and then they began to ask me questions about what the rest of the world was like, what America was like, about my family. They had seen my son on television. They were asking me about him and we became good friends and even exchanged addresses. I left going back into the streets with the cross as they said, "We'll spread the word. No problem, Preacher, no problem."

I will never forget one lovely lady, whose address I somehow lost, but she runs the old wrecking yard where you buy parts from old cars. She had me in for tea and we spent such a lovely time together. Another home that I was in was a minister who directs an interdenominational youth movement called "Youth Alive." He grabbed me and said, "I know who you are. We once had Rosey Grier, the famous American football player, former bodyguard for American presidential candidate Bobby Kennedy and now a committed preacher for Jesus Christ." I had a lovely meal in that minister's home with all of his family. There was crowd after crowd that was gathering as I preached over and over again. It's a day that I will never forget and a day that I'm sure the people will never forget as a white man walked with the cross through Soweto. I arrived at a police station. A large crowd of people were gathered around me and I preached, praying with them and leading many to receive Christ. They were all watching me. Would I go to the police station, or would I avoid it? The large police station was all black policemen and they were standing back from the fence probably feeling certain that I would not come to them because for some people, to be a friend with the police, is to automatically become their enemy. But Jesus did not discriminate against the authorities of His day even when He healed the Roman Centurion's son. I knew that this was one of the most important things I would do all day because there is much hatred directed toward the police in Soweto. I walked with the cross straight toward the station and up to the gate. Two guards standing there were looking at me in startled amazement. I gave them "Jesus" stickers with a picture of the cross on it saying, "Smile, God loves you." Other police began to gather. Soon when they saw that I was not their enemy but that I loved them just as I loved the people outside, dozens of police gathered and I preached to them sharing the love of Jesus Christ, how we are to be kind, peacemakers, we're to love our neighbors as ourselves. I shared the same message - that Jesus washes away our sins and can give new life and can make us one with the people that I had shared with across the street. I then asked if they would pray. Everyone took off their hat and bowed with me. When I finished, they began to ask questions. They couldn't believe that I was actually in Soweto. But the most amazing thing, they couldn't believe that I would speak to them because they felt that everyone hated them and they began to share their hurts - that they had families and children and they were threatened at all times with death in their families. And I could feel their suffering as well as the suffering of the crowds outside.

The man who was perhaps the commanding officer looked at me and said, "Now what are you going to do?" I said, "What do you mean?" He said, "You can't go back out there now that they see that you are our friend." And I said, "Certainly I will go back." I said, "Jesus loves everybody, no matter who they are or what side they're on or what they've done. There must be peace and to have peace, I must go to all sides." They said they would be praying for me and I walked across the street where a huge crowd had gathered. I gave them the same kind of stickers I had been giving to the police, "Smile, God loves you." I preached to them the same message I had preached to the police with no problem.

Finally, the day came to an end and then the night as I slept in a family's home. I had walked through Soweto. The cross had gone through another place of critical need by the grace of God. I was filled with emotions, joy, beauty and peace; and hurt, sadness, and pain. But so is life on this earth and the way of the cross.

Namibia
Southwest Africa

January 1, 1986 - Windhoek

Well, I lived to see a New Year and I am here in the desert getting ready to leave with the cross. I feel the pain of deep passion for the world but a joy to go on in even more radical living. "It's further back than ahead."

Okahandja

What a day! I tell you, if all of 1986 is like this, it's awesome. My driver carrying all our gospel material is named Peter. He is from a local tribe here and a wonderful man. The glory of God was all around the city and along the road, all races gathering around the cross. As I walked through the city of Windhoek, we gave out thousands of gospel tracts and stickers and I preached over and over. Tonight we sleep in a little home almost eaten up with mosquitoes.

Next Day

Oh, it is hot! I saw the sky turn brown. It was a sandstorm. Indescribable. I crawled under a bridge and covered my face with my shirt. The sand was choking and blinding. All traffic stopped. Then there was a flood of rain for about three or four minutes. Then it was all over and the most beautiful double rainbow filled the sky. It's the most beautiful I've ever seen. It was so bright and stunning.

I was on the front page of the English newspaper in this predominantly German and Afrikaans speaking country. South West was a former German colony before World War I and then became a South African protectorate. There is great controversy and a war that is being fought concerning its independence. But here, the facilities - its hotels, etc. - are mostly multiracial.

Swakopmund

Well, it is hot, hot, hot! The road is steaming hot. Hot wind. I drink hot water. I'm baked almost black from the sun. The Namibia Desert is the oldest desert in the world but all along this road cars and trucks have been stopping. I have led so many men to Jesus. It's mostly big ranches and mines out here and very kind people who have a barbecue which they call a 'braai' which they prepare most nights for me.

The nights out here in the desert in the Southern Hemisphere are, without a doubt, the most glorious in the world. I have been getting up and walking at 4:00 o'clock in the morning so that I get two-and-a-half hours of walking through the desert with the cross at night before the daylight.

Namibia Desert

What a fabulous day of witnessing in the desert. From the normal temperature of 115 degrees out in the desert, here by the seaside, it is very cold. I actually had to wear a coat. There is a thick, wet fog and a strong wind. I preached four times today at local African churches. One meeting was at a local Dutch Reformed Colored Church.

Walvis Bay

What a glorious day through the desert with the highest sand dunes in the world on one side reaching up to 3,000 feet high and the cold Atlantic Ocean on the other side with the water currents coming up from the South Pole. The people in South West are some of the greatest I've ever known and the beauty of this desert country is wonderful.

Capetown

Today, I met Reverend Allan Boesak at this church where he is pastor. He is also the President of the World Council of Reformed Churches, Chaplain to the University in Capetown and Head of the UDF Party. He has just been released from three months in prison where he was in detention. He was waiting outside the church to greet me. Accompanying me was Reverend Neville McDonald. We went into his office where we were seated and he asked me about my work with the cross, about the response of the people and what I had been seeing in South Africa. I gave him my book, "Arthur, A Pilgrim" and he gave me one of his books. Then I asked about his life with Christ. He said there had been a great renewal within his life in the past few months, especially during the time he had been in prison. He spoke of how Christ was so real to him now. He talked about his early life and how difficult it is oftentimes to bring hope and comfort to those who have suffered injustices and been discriminated against under the apartheid system. Even though he is one of the top political leaders in

South Africa, we only talked about Jesus. I remember looking at him as I could read in his eyes that he was wondering what direction our visit would take. I read to him these words from Revelation 1:9: "I, John, who am also your brother and companion in tribulation and in the kingdom and patience of Jesus Christ, was in the Isle that is called Patmos, for the word of God, and for the testimony of Jesus Christ." I said, "I have only come as your companion in Christ. Relax. I am not here to debate you, or to advise you, or to drain you, only to lift up your hand in the name of Jesus and pray for you and share hope, love and joy. Jesus is the answer. May our lives reflect Him to the troubled world as we seek to establish justice, equality and God's kingdom in the hearts of all the people." He shared with me his struggle to seek to live out the teachings of Jesus. After two hours, we decided to have prayer. He came around from behind his desk and knelt down beside me. He gripped my hand with his two hands as we prayed. We both wept. It was wonderful. I understood his struggles and he understood mine. We both shared a level of understanding and love that transcended our spoken words.

Crossroads squatter camp

Today, I carried the cross through Crossroads, the black squatter camp located near the Capetown airport. The government has tried to tear down the temporary shelters as it is considered an illegal settlement with no sewage or water, etc. But it has been strongly resisted by the local inhabitants. Much conflict with the police and army and also great conflict for territory between the different black African tribes that collect there with local headmen or chiefs controlling various sections. Crossroads and Soweto are probably the most well known trouble spots in South Africa. Yet today, I walked through there with the cross. There was a special reconciliation prayer group that met at the local hospital clinic sponsored by the Christian churches. There were eighteen men there, representing all the racial and religious groupings of the area. They invited me to have prayer with them. Their mission is reconciliation but when I suggested that they walk out the door with me into troubled Crossroads, there seemed to be complete panic. "Why, it's dangerous. We would be killed." Every excuse imaginable. But I said, "I have only found people gathering in peace around the cross." I said in love and kindness, "Do as you feel led but I must go with the cross." Not one black, or colored, or Indian in that group dared to walk into that sea of shacks to bring reconciliation, but three white men did, including my dear friend and businessman, Mr. John Bridgeman. It seemed to me that the reconciliation group only wants to be with those who are already reconciled. However, in the horrible physical conditions of Crossroads, the people were so lovely to me. No problem at all. Crowds gathered as we preached, gave out Jesus stickers and then I took a group of men to a store and bought food as they said, "We can't find a job. We've only eaten white bread and no meat for weeks." It was one of the most beautiful days I have ever spent. And when the severe fighting and killing broke out a few months later, I wonder what happened to all my friends there.

Capetown

Wow! What a day! What a year! I am awake at 4:00 a.m. I can't sleep. I'm so tired. I'm exhausted. This morning, I preached at the Good Hope Christian Center that meets at Three Arts Theater. It is a new fellowship, only a year-and-a-half old, completely multiracial with congregation, band, choir and pastors. They run about 3,000 people each meeting. A young couple, Neville and Wendy McDonald are the main pastors. It was a glorious gathering. Many of their people walked with me and the cross as I arrived in Capetown. Tonight, I preached at the most important Dutch Reformed Afrikaans speaking church in all of South Africa. It is the church where most of the South African government cabinet regularly attend, including President Botha. The pastor, Dr. Ernst Van Der Walt is a beautiful man of God and I have had great fellowship with he and his wife and lovely children. I'll never forget as I carried the cross into the church. The Dutch Reform in South Africa are ultra conservative, usually with no cross in their building. The minister is always in suit and tie and his hair is certainly not as long as mine. Their meetings are conducted only in Afrikaans, even though most people also could speak English, so it was indeed a revolutionary thing to be invited to preach there and to come carrying the cross into the worship service, of course, without a suit and tie. The pastor led me into the church saying, "Follow me." I preached in the power of the Holy Spirit sharing the message of Christ, of salvation, of His unity and peace, and of my walk and ministry among all the peoples of all races in South Africa. I concluded with an invitation for people to receive Christ. Then the pastor dismissed in prayer and I stepped down from the platform. The people were turning quietly to leave. Then spontaneously, just as if it had been planned, the entire congregation turned to the front, rushed toward me and began to sing in English, "We Love you in the Love of the Lord." They began to raise their hands and praise the Lord. I was weeping. It was one of the most beautiful things I have ever seen. I said, "You've sung me a song. Now let me sing you a song," and I sang them one of the songs I had written, "Thou Art a Flower to Me." I was weeping and smiling and so were they. For over an hour, we were bathed in the glory of the Lord. What a way to end this trip of carrying the cross in South Africa!

Day before yesterday, I was with Allan Boesak considered by many to be a radical leader. Yesterday, I walked in Crossroads even as it was under marshal law and then preached in the main park in downtown Capetown. This morning, I preached at a multiracial church and tonight, I preached in the most influential church in South Africa in a denomination that has traditionally, though it is changing, been the major proponent of the apartheid system. Who could believe such a schedule! I have been with the richest and the poorest, the most radical and the most conservative, all in the last three days. God has led us through South Africa since October. Now I'll see my family soon.

Giyani, Capital of Gazankulu

This is where I am to be. After meeting Brother Piet Mabunda in the park in Johannesburg and giving him that special ring, I now arrived to carry the cross through his area. They were very excited at my arrival. This is a totally black area and it feels so wonderful to be among them. At my arrival in his village called Ngobe, he had me immediately carry the cross through their neighborhood. They have electricity and now running water only installed last week. This is great progress for them as construction and development is going on everywhere changing this area from a sleepy African village to modern new shopping centers and beautiful homes. Many were converted in the front yard of his home the first night. The next day, we walked

into Giyani. Then more crowds welcomed us and I preached
many times. Tonight at our meeting in the open air for
the first time, all the churches of this area came
together. The various churches had been very non-
cooperative with each other but now they all gathered
around the cross. We had a great crowd as many walked
for miles to come. It was awesome as the sea of faces
filled the front yard and bodies packed together. As I
was sitting in a chair just before I preached, I saw one
of the most beautiful views. Directly in front of me was
the cross; secondly, masses of people all around the
cross - even into the darkness; thirdly, the clear
quarter moon in a sky full of stars. I have never seen a
more beautiful sight. I thought the cross represented
the gift of salvation, my love for Jesus and my life on
the roads. Secondly, the masses of people, their faces
smiling, eager, represented the world. I love them all.
Thirdly, the moon and the stars represented the glory of
God in the universe and my love for the beauty of
nature. Many were saved and many were healed and as I
went to bed in this lovely family's home, there were
African drums beating and people chanting. It was like
an all night disco! Ha!

Malanulele

What a day! Up at 6:00 a.m. and on the road. Piet
took off from work and drove for me and interpreted. He
is just great. Crowds gathered all along the road. Many
people were healed. One man who had been in great pain
for years was healed. He went and got his sick wife and
she too was healed. Two policemen stopped and were
talking to us. One was a preacher, the other was
unsaved. I led the one policeman to Christ and he said,
"I want to quit smoking but I can't. I spend most of my
money on cigarettes." I said, "Where do you keep your

cigarettes?" He pointed to his shirt pocket. I went to the Landrover and got a pocket Bible and put it where the cigarettes had been. We all began to laugh and he said, "I think this is better." I spent the night with a local evangelist and his house filled with people so we had to have another meeting. That made sixteen meetings for the day and I had walked twenty-five miles. I lay here in the penthouse which is a simple tent that folds up on top of this truck. I am now using the Landrover that we imported from Europe and has been outfitted as a four-wheel drive camper with built-in P.A. system, beds for four including a refrigerator, stove and sink. And I can carry an awesome amount of gospel material to give away.

The road is now dirt as I go into the homeland country of Venda. The buses and trucks throw up a blinding amount of dirt as they pass.

Selebi-Phikwe - Country of Botswana

When I was coming out of Soweto last Christmas, I met a wonderful minister from this town. They have a very good church where they help feed the poor children, teach typing and various community services as well as preach the full gospel. The pastor Reverend D. T. Monaheng had invited me when I came back to South Africa to come and see them. I drove over to their city which is a new mining town located at the edge of the Kalahari Desert. When I arrived at the church, there were children everywhere. Mrs. Monaheng greeted me and was so excited that I had come. But the pastor was gone evangelizing in another country for two weeks. We gathered all the children together and I preached to them and then she said, "Yesterday some people brought a paralyzed child to us from one of the villages. We prayed for the child last night. He is about twelve years old. He is lame in his right arm and right leg for four years. You must come and pray for him." I took the cross down from the Landrover and we walked through the streets. There at a house, I prayed for this boy. His arm had no use, but as I prayed, he was completely healed and for the first time in four years, he could bend his arm and hold a piece of bread between his fingers and eat. We walked around the yard and he used his hand perfectly. Going back to the church, word spread and there were people waiting to be saved. I was only there for two days, but it was glorious. It was very strange that in this short trip, I went through five army road blocks where everything in the Landrover had to be unloaded in the boiling sun and the vehicle was thoroughly searched. Some road blocks were only a few miles from the next. It was good to get back into South Africa where I never saw a road block in eight months or was ever searched coming or going, not even at the airports.

Thaba Nchu - Country of Bophuthatswana

As I carried the cross through this area of the country, I was greeted with tremendous response as crowds gathered. They were so eager to hear the message of Jesus. Everyone, it seemed, wanted me to spend the night with them.

Maseru - Country of Lesotho

As I walked through this capital city and toward the interior of this mountain land, the response was very great, especially the children. They would gather and I would preach and sing and they would sing. I remember one car that stopped and a teen-age Indian girl

came up. Her father is a professor at the university
here but she saw me and heard me preach at the YMCA in
Cochen, India last year. I remember one night here in
the mountains, it was minus 9 celsius (or 15 F). There
was ice and snow and it is very beautiful but extremely
poor country.

A Mountain Valley in the Country of Transkei

Just south of Rama's Gate, is a beautiful valley
coming down from the mountains. It was so responsive -
mostly women and children because the men have left for
the cities to work. This is one of the major problems in
South Africa - the men go away and work returning only
for short times during the year. But I was so well
received here. I had been buying and giving away much
food in all of this area as well as gospel material.
These were a very loving people.

Durban - Last Day in South Africa

I spent the night with my good friends, Richard and
Lorine Scallan. My plane was leaving on the night of
August 21 to London. A bishop, David Pytches, an
Anglican minister, who served in South America and is
now at St. Andrews Church in Chorleywood, England and
his wife and another couple arrived just before I was
leaving to stay at the Scallans. We sat talking about
the great move of God's Spirit in South Africa and about
how to listen to the voice of the Holy Spirit. Then I
spoke about worshipping in spirit and in truth. The
glory of God was so strong. We all were on the floor
praying, weeping and praising God. It seemed as if my
heart would tear out as I remembered all my friends and
the things that I had seen. I remembered the words of
Jesus in Luke 10:23,24, "And He turned to His disciples

and said privately, 'Blessed are the eyes which see the things that you see; For I tell you, that many prophets and kings have desired to see those things which you see, and have not seen them; and to hear those things which you hear, and have not heard them." I left weeping, and yet rejoicing. My Landrover is still there and I am returning in December, God willing, with Paul Crouch to open the television station in Ciskei.

I am sitting beside the beach in South Florida as God has instructed me to write this book even before I get home to Los Angeles. Two of my children - Joy, 17 and Jerusalem, 6 - are with me here even as my heart misses the people and the children - especially the children - of South Africa.

Poems Written in South Africa

The South of Africa
Grips me....
Where did the world go...!!

* * * * * * * * *

The fast
        mixes with
The slow....
I look back to where I've been....
Glance ahead to where I may go....
        and
        'wonder' --
And feel the 'glory' --
And the 'pain'
And smile through the tears....
        of
        joy and sadness!
But you can only
        cry
If you've loved a lot.
So I have a steady flow
Even if you can't see them
        And my riches I carry
        Not in my pocket
        Or put in a bank
        But carry my riches in my heart
            And
            I
        smile....

* * * * * * * * *

Well, time moves on
And so does many strange things
We grow older
The rains come - the clouds float away
Dawn comes - the day
            and then
            the night
The tide comes in as it always has
Snow falls in the high mountains
And human cruelty is as modern
            as it is ancient
What have we learned in the past 5,000 years?
Are we less murderous?
Have we laid down the instruments of war?
Or developed faster ways of killing?
Are we more Forgiving?
            Loving?
            Moral?
            Godly?
Has time developed the better nature of humanity?
I look at Jesus and dream....

                * * * * * * * * *

By lamp light -
Under a star filled sky -- I write
And smile,
After a hot day and now a cool night
I sit,
Feet burn, body needs massage -
            and it seems
            a
            long way
            from every place
            but
            Here!

The cross! the cross!
Dust flies up from hundreds of feet---
The heat bears down
I sweat
I preach
My throat is dry
We pray
Heaven and people rejoice
Questions are asked
Stickers about Jesus and gospel papers are given
The cross moves on
Borne on weary shoulders and feet
But a smile
"Oh I love you Lord
Thanks for letting me bear thy cross and good
                                    news to the world"
A truck passes and dust chokes me
Then it settles and I see a crowd waiting --
The scene changes - again and again:
But the rhythm is the same
And I press on --
          To that next village
That next auto to stop
That next face --
Till I see --- 'His' --- face
          face to face

                    * * * * * * * * *

South Africa
The answer is so simple -
The solution is easy -
          Love
But the pride is so binding.

                    * * * * * * * * *

There are many choices....
           But
Only one - PRIORITY!
                'The Father's business'

                * * * * * * * * *

I lay here with so many feelings
Thoughts race
And emotions flash over me
Sadness and joy become one
I want to express...and to hide
To be known and unknown
I am Godly
Yet human
           flesh
            but
           spirit
A dreamer
and
A realist
           a bit of all the
           places I've been
           of all the people I've known
I know the earth like most people know their town
Hello becomes --- good-bye
Postcards take the place of flesh, and
Anyone who said they knew me, would be a fool
So I lay here with so many feelings
Thoughts race -
And emotions flash over me.

                * * * * * * * * *

Information and Observations

There is a very great spiritual awakening taking place in South Africa. There are many multiracial churches here. Many Anglican churches are experiencing great awakening as well as Methodist and Dutch Reform. The Dutch Reform Church has been the main proponent of apartheid but this is changing very fast. Through each of the racial areas, black, white, Indian and colored, there is a mighty revival taking place. Three fairly new evangelical church groups that are completely multiracial and growing at an astounding rate are the Rhema Churches, the Hatfield Community Churches and the Christian Centers, the latter three being more popularly known as Charismatic churches. There are many independent groups that are experiencing great growth and response. One of the greatest meetings while I was in South Africa was at a Catholic Monastery called Mariannhill located just outside Durban where a very saintly sister ministers in evangelism - Sister Agnes alone with Father Lautensehloger. As I carried the cross into there and preached, we were all weeping and greatly moved by the power of God. Many churches are alive and on the move in South Africa. The one thing that all groups in South Africa have in common is the cross. I have seen the unity of the cross in the midst of the troubles. If only we could stay at the feet of Jesus and live like Him. Because of this 'Jesus reservoir', South Africa has some of the most racially tolerant people in the world. As of now, there is nothing like a race war in South Africa. There is much goodwill among all the people toward each other. The streets are filled with children on bicycles, single ladies driving along the roads. There are all the ingredients necessary for a solution. I am optimistic for the future if we will keep our eyes on Jesus.

* * * * * * * *

There has been, in my opinion, a very evil system that is known more recently as apartheid that has sought to divide and keep the people in their own racial groupings. This system began in the colonial days and became more rigid in the last thirty or so years. This system is failing fast. The last days I was in Durban, they integrated the swimming pools. Now that may not seem much but I grew up in Mississippi and Louisiana in the 1950's and 1960's and anyone that has lived through the breakdown of the segregation system in the U.S. south knows what this means. The marriage laws have been changed to allow inter-racial marriages and the list goes on and on and I see things changing in the last two or three years faster than the Old South changed in the same period of time. But South Africa has much further to go because it is so deeply rooted in the segregated housing patterns and racial classifications and so on. I grieve about the constant injustice. The blacks in the Republic of South Africa still do not have voting rights but as I have lived throughout the country almost all the people of all races now want change, justice and equality. Everyone must support that change and seek the complete abolition of the past evil system. As we look at Jesus, we see the model of how all people are to be. I oppose the evil apartheid system but I support the people of South Africa and love them with all my heart.

Now hear me carefully, after walking across South Africa, sitting in prayer and fasting in the city centers for twenty-one days, not one person has asked me to pray against the economy and for the closing down of jobs in South Africa. But I have had thousands of people asking me to pray for them to get a job or to get a better job or expressing their need and desire for better clothes, better houses, better health services, better schools. You could never, if you held the children in your arms and saw the faces of the people and been in their homes, favor putting them out of work and starving them to death. I have had wonderful Christian businessmen weeping as they have told me of having to lay off hundreds of workers because of the boycotts from other nations and seeing this create unemployment, hunger and loss of dignity.

The South African farming system is very delicate. In many places it takes ten years or longer to grow a strong bunch of grass. The operations of mines are very intricate. It seems so strange that much of the world is raising billions of dollars to feed the starving in North and Central Africa, trying to help them grow food, stop overgrazing and become industrialized. And yet these same people want to destroy the best developed agricultural and industrial areas in Africa and add thirty million more people to the starvation list, not counting the millions of other people and the surrounding African states that are dependent upon the South African agricultural, industrial and transportation systems. We have too much hate in the world. We don't need more hate. We need more love. We need to love the people of South Africa and help them. Let's oppose injustice but support the people. Let's give massive aid to develop new schools and well educated teachers especially in black areas. If one wants to help the blacks then put factories and development programs in South Africa with black management. Let's pour aid into helping the children, the needy, building hospitals, irrigation systems. Let's help the people rather than destroy them. Our United States farmers supply Russia with much of their food supported by American taxpayer subsidiaries. The U.S. government opposes the Soviet system yet we feed them even as missiles are pointed at us. We believe in freedom of religion but our strongest ally in the Arab world, Saudia Arabia, refuses any freedom of religion except Islam. The United States believes in separation of church and state, yet we support Israel which is a religious Jewish State and England where the King or Queen is also head of the Church. We can oppose injustice in South Africa but still help the people. Perhaps I have seen the people of South Africa and lived with them and fallen in love with them of all races. I see their needs, hopes and dreams in a very personal and non-political way. I don't think you can condemn me for this because the very mark of the teachings of Jesus was, "I was hungry and you gave Me meat; I was thirsty and you gave Me drink; I was a stranger and you took Me in; naked and you clothed Me; sick and you visited Me; in prison and you came to Me."

THE PRESS

The South African newspapers, radio and television have been very open and truthful about my trips. I have been well treated factually and in spirit by all the press. We were on the South African news. Joshua spoke on a program called Video II. In February, South African TV broadcast a half-an-hour special as they spent several days filming our walk into Johannesburg. They used my voice as the only commentary and showed me with all the people in complete honesty. My message and lifestyle was not compromised at all. They said it was one of the most popular programs ever filmed by them and they did not receive one telephone call or letter of criticism. When we returned for the prayer and fasting, they spent weeks with us day and night and have now aired and given to me a one-half-hour program that shows in film many of the things that I have written about in this book including the crowds, the prayers, the weepings, dramatic healings and the footwashings and so on. I would like to thank them for their desire to make known the truth of what we had been seeing in the streets to all of the nation. I feel that I must be the most loved person by all people in South Africa.

I must add one further point. Although I do not find pleasure in saying this, I feel it is necessary in conveying the truth of my experiences. The western news press that is in South Africa has absolutely no interest in anything peaceful or objective. Had I fasted against something, instead of for love, peace and reconciliation, I would have been on the western news. We had thousands washing each other's feet. This was not news. While the western press reported all public meetings in South Africa banned, I, along with a total of tens of thousands of other people combined, gathered publicly twenty-four hours a day in the heart of the three largest cities. They knew we were there. They walked by with their cameras and sometimes even mocked us. I remember one reporter from a western newspaper who said, "We are not interested in this kind of gathering. We are only interested in the troubles. This is not news." Somehow if ten people gather to protest something, it's news. If 5,000 blacks and whites gather together to praise the Lord and love each other, this is not news. The picture of South Africa as presently being in a blood bath is as distorted as taking the crime figures of Los Angles and saying this is all there is in Los Angeles. The American people live daily with more terror from maniac gunmen, serial killers, robbers, muggers, rapists and sexual perverts. The normal South African community has much less violence than where I live in the San Fernando Valley of Los Angeles where two ladies have been stabbed and sexually assaulted directly in front of our house; my daughter was robbed at gun point a few feet from my front yard and my son, Joshua, who has never had any personal violence or threats toward him in all our time in South Africa, was robbed at knife point near our house. And the police have come to every home in the neighborhood including my house, and warned us not to let our children out at night. We are also trying to bring that type situation to an end by sharing Christ in our neighborhood. But I simply want to emphasize that our little part of a residential neighborhood doesn't make world news because it is so common across America. Perhaps one must understand something about the western news media. We speak of freedom of press but our press is in no wise free. It's very existence is to make money. If a news program is number one, it may sell it's commercials for, say half a million dollars per minute. If it has a low news rating, it can only sell it's advertising for a quarter of a million dollars per minute. If there is no conflict the western press must create conflict or emphasize it. Take for instance our most popular news and current events programs like Phil Donahue or Ted Koppell. Their very intent is to emphasize divisions, heighten antagonism and create conflict. Ted Koppell will put on two or three people in the guise of objectivity but the purpose is to create anger and conflict so that people will keep watching. I have seen this from seventeen years of walking around the world. Whether it has been in

Lebanon, Israel, Poland, El Salvador, Nicaragua, Northern Ireland and so on. As a group, most western reporters are either atheists or skeptics and spend most of their time in the hotels at the bar discussing conflict and ignoring anything like good news - making heroes out of hijackers, terrorists and agitators - while ignoring the simple people of peace. Perhaps one of the greatest contributions in this world to conflict, fear and confusion, is the western press. Jesus said, "Blessed are the peacemakers."

Peace in the Holy Bible

"Blessed are the peacemakers for they shall be called the children of God." Matthew 5:9

"Love the truth and peace." Zechariah 8:19

"Have peace one with another." Mark 9:50

Glory to God in the highest and on earth peace, goodwill toward men." Luke 2:14

"If it be possible as much as lies in you, live peaceably with all men." Romans 12:18

"For God is not the author of confusion, but of peace." I Corinthians 14:33

"Live in peace, and the God of love and peace shall be with you." II Corinthians 13:11

"That we may lead a quiet and peaceful life in all godliness and honesty." I Timothy 2:2

"Follow peace with all men and holiness, without which no man shall see the Lord." Hebrews 12:14

"The fruit of righteousness is sown in peace of them that make peace." James 3:18

"Let him flee evil and do good; let him seek peace, and ensue it." I Peter 3:11

"I am for peace: but when I speak, they are for war."
Psalm 120:7

"To the counselors of peace there is joy." Proverbs
12:20

"He shall be called Wonderful, Counselor, the Mighty
God, the Everlasting Father, The Prince of Peace.:
Isaiah 9:6

"And they shall beat their swords into ploughshares, and
their spears into pruninghooks; nation shall not lift up
sword against nation, neither shall they learn war
anymore." Isaiah 2:4

"Peace I leave with you, my peace I give to you; not as
the world giveth give I you. Let not your heart be
troubled, neither let it be afraid." John 14:27

"Jesus came and stood in the midst and said, 'Peace be
unto you'." John 20:19

"Therefore being justified by faith, we have peace with
God through our Lord Jesus Christ." Romans 5:1

"For He is our peace who hath made both one, and hath
broken down the middle wall of partition between us;
having abolished in His flesh the enmity, even the law
of commandments contained in ordinances; for to make in
Himself of two, one new man, so making peace; And that
He might reconcile both unto God in one body by the
cross, having slain the enmity thereby: And came and
preached peace to you that were afar off and to them
that were near." Ephesians 2:14-17

"But the fruit of the Spirit is love, joy, peace, long-suffering, gentleness, goodness, faith, meekness, and self-control." Galatians 5:22

"And having made peace through the blood of His cross by Him to reconcile all things unto Himself." Colossians 1:20

"And let the peace of God rule in your hearts." Colossians 3:15

"Now the Lord of peace Himself give you peace always by all means." II Thessalonians 3:16

Hatred in the Holy Bible

"You've heard that it hath been said you shall love thy neighbor and hate your enemy but I say unto you love your enemies, bless them that curse you, do good to them that hate you, and pray for them that despitefully use you and persecute you." Matthew 5:43,44

If you forgive not men their trespasses, neither will your Father forgive your trespasses." Matthew 6:15

"Let all bitterness, and wrath, and anger, and clamor, and evil speaking, be put away from you, with all malice." Ephesians 4:31

"But now also put off all these; anger, wrath, malice, blasphemy, filthy communication out of your mouth." Colossians 3:8

"He that saith he is in the light and hateth his brother, is in darkness." I John 2:9

"He that loveth not his brother abideth in death. Whoever hateth his brother is a murderer: and you know that no murderer hath eternal life abiding in him." I John 3:14,15

"If a man say, I love God, and hateth his brother, he is a liar; for he that loveth not his brother whom he hath seen, how can he love God whom he hath not seen?" I John 4:20

"You have heard that it hath been said, An eye for an eye, and a tooth for a tooth; but I say unto you, that you resist not evil; but whosoever shall smite you on your right cheek, turn to him the other also. And if any man will sue you at the law, and take away your coat, let him have your cloak also. And whosoever shall compel you to go a mile, go with him two. Give to him that asketh you, and from him that would borrow of you turn not away. You have heard that it hath been said, You shall love your neighbor and hate your enemy. But I say unto you, Love your enemies, bless them that curse you, do good to them that hate you, and pray for them which despitefully use you, and persecute you." Matthew 5: 38-44.

"And they went, and entered into a village of the Samaritans, to make ready for him. And they did not receive Him, because his face was as though He would go to Jerusalem. And when His disciples James and John saw this, they said, Lord, will You that we command fire to come down from heaven and consume them, even as Elias did? But He turned, and rebuked them, and said, You know not what manner of spirit you are of. For the Son of Man is not come to destroy men's live, but to save them." Luke 9:52-56.

"Recompense to no man evil for evil." Romans 12:17

"Vengeance is Mine; I will repay, saith the Lord." Romans 12:19

Blessed are the Peacemakers

After having walked with the cross through twenty wars in the world in places as divergent as Nicaragua and Chad from Northern Ireland to Beirut and so on and having been in jail twenty times, been beaten, stoned, been before a firing squad to be shot. Had the cross stolen, broken and spit upon. I've seen tribes fighting with spears in Papua, New Guinea and planes dive bombing in Lebanon and having eaten, slept and walked among army troops and guerrilla fighters all over the world. I have some observations that I feel are relevant to the root of the conflicts of our time.

* * *

We are living today in a world of escalating violence, the cycle of death, hate and revenge seems to be without end. When you speak to one side and then the other, they tell a story of past injustices and bloodshed that is also happening now. The atrocities of yesterday, 50 years ago or 400 years ago all blend into one. Memory, instead of bringing wisdom and compassion, is the fuel to feed the fire of hate and vengeance. Instead of the sore being healed it still festers with the deadly poison, exploding in violence. The Klu Klux Klan can burn crosses, still filled with the hate of 2,000 years ago and miss the true meaning of the cross. Both Jew and Palestinian can give complete justification for every act of violence. Catholic and Protestant in Northern Ireland can morally justify their "Godly" behavior. Blacks have very true stories of discrimination and slavery, the whites can tell you of black mobs that have gone on a rampage. Iraq and Iran both Muslim but of two different sects continue a blood bath, both justified in their own eyes. A fanatical young man lobs grenades into a church or a synagogue with a clear conscience because he has absorbed past perceived injustices and present revenge. A fighter pilot unloads his weapons of death upon innocent people below with no sign of remorse. His conscience is clear, he only followed a command -- as all of Hitlers death agents said -- or the soldiers who crucified Christ. Sikh rises against Hindus in Punjab, Buddhists struggle against Tamil Hindu's in Sri Lanka, Korean resentment of past occupation by Japan is still explosive, peasants exploited by big landlords and communist threatened by capitalist. Self-justification of your hatred cannot be justified by events of the past, whether they be the crucifixion of Christ or the holocaust. We must let go of hurt less it become hate and consume us in the inferno. Where is the end? In order to see the end you must see the beginning. Satan seeking revenge against God, deceived Adam and Eve. Cain rose up and slew Abel. God is the author of life. Satan is the author of death. Jesus made it clear when he said "The thief has come to steal and to kill and destroy, I am come that they might have life, and that they might have it more abundantly." John 10:10 We are the victims of Satans revenge against God. Look what he has done in his savage revenge in the world around us. The revenge can be broken! Something has gone wrong, sin. Something has gone right, Jesus. We don't have to live in Satan's revenge, we can be free. South Africa can be free from vengeance, death and hate. So can Palestine and Israel, Lebanon, Christians and Jews and Muslims, for at the cross peace was made. Through Jesus Christ and His shed blood, sinful man can have peace with God. At the cross the worst of man met the best of God. For at the cross all people can gather together, injustices can be laid aside. Hatred and prejudices can be cleansed and we can become new, for the cross not only was a place of death but through the resurrection of Christ has become the place of hope. As Jesus said, "Father, forgive them, for they know not what they do." Yet peace must begin with a person becoming right with God, then one can find peace with their family or husband or wife or children and their neighbors, then their community and world. Dear friend, if you don't have peace in your own heart, how can you have peace in the world? With our earth being ravaged by broken homes of marriage, where a man and a woman cannot live together in the same house with the children of their own blood, how do we think that we can have peace between warring factions on earth when the war is already in our own homes and our own hearts and the first casualty is our own children? Both on a personal basis and as society we must experience forgiveness and reconciliation. Yet, the world races headlong into madness. STOP, CONSIDER, you can't create hate to create good, you can't seek revenge and build understanding, you can't say I love God and hate your brother. In the name of morality we are teaching the world to hate. You don't overcome evil with evil. Mrs. Coretta King, widow of the slain U.S. civil rights leader during her recent visit to South Africa said, "One cannot use immoral means to achieve moral goals." Some people try to get you to hate South Africa so that it will be a better place but you don't build love on hate. The provocation of hate in the name of justice is the ultimate of deception. When you receive Christ into your life you take on His attributes, when you don't know God you take on the attributes of Satan. As Jesus once said to some religious leaders of His day, "You are of your father, the devil." John 8:44

What did Jesus say about forgiveness? "You have heard that it has been said an eye for an eye, a tooth for a tooth but I say unto you that you resist not evil, but whosoever shall smite thee upon thy cheek turn to him the other also and if any man shall sue thee in the law and take away thy coat, let him have your cloak also. For whosoever shall compel thee to go a mile go with him two. Give to him that ask thee and from him that would borrow of thee turn not away. You have heard that it had been said thou shalt love thy neighbor and hate thy enemy. But I say unto you, love thy enemy, bless them that curse you, do good to them that hate you and pray for them which despitefully use you and persecute you. That you may be called the children of your Father which is in heaven. For He maketh the sun to rise on the evil and on the good and sendeth rain on the just and the unjust. If you love them which love you what reward have you? Do not even the publicans the same? And if you salute your brother in honor what do you do more than others? Do not even the publicans also? But be ye therefore perfect even as your father which is in heaven is perfect." (Matthew 5:38-48) Jesus even puts the responsibility upon the one who has been wronged. Even if we are guiltless and have done nothing wrong we have the responsibility of reconciliation. Jesus said, "therefore if you bring your gift to the altar and there remember that thy brother hath ought against thee, leave there thy gift before the altar and go thy way. First be reconciled to thy brother and then come and offer thy gift." (Matthew 5:23-24) God does not even want your money unless you are reconciled to your brother. Then God will accept your gift. In the Lord's prayer, we are to forgive those who have trespassed against us as God forgives our trespasses. The true peacemaker is not to be the cause of more suffering and hatred but is to be seen in this light. (Matthew 25:41-46) "Then shall He say unto them on His left hand, depart from Me you cursed into everlasting fire prepared for the devil and his angels for I was hungry and you gave Me no meat, I was thirsty and you gave Me no drink, I was a stranger and you took Me not in, naked and you clothed Me not, sick and imprisoned and you visited Me not. Then shall they also answer him saying Lord when so all were You hungry or thirsty, or a stranger, or naked, or sick, or imprisoned and did not minister unto You, then shall He answer them. I say unto you in so much as you did it not to one of the lest of these, you did it not to Me. And these shall go away into everlasting punishment, but the righteous into life eternal."

Let us assume the role of peacemaker. Dr. O. S. Hawkins, my dear friend says, "Jesus said 'blessed are the peacemakers.' He did not say blessed are the peace lovers. It is one thing to say peace, it is another to go into the conflict and reach out with one hand to the one side and the other hand to the other side." The true peacemaker tries to reconcile not agitate. The way of the peacemaker is simple: love, forgiveness and reconciliation.

"All things are of God who has reconciled us to himself by Jesus Christ and hath given to us the ministry of reconciliation. To wit that God was in Christ reconciling the world unto himself. Not imputing their trespasses unto them and have committed them to us, the word of reconciliation. Now then, we are ambassadors for Christ as though God did beseech you by us we pray you in Christ stead be you reconciled to God. For He hath made Him to be sin for us who knew no sin that we may be made the righteousness of God in Him." (II Corinthians 5:18-21)

Perhaps the clear desire of Jesus as expressed at His birth by the angels, "Peace on earth, good will to men" is seen in His words "and the glory which thou gave Me, I have given them that they may be one even as we are one." (John 17:22) When we receive his glory we are one family of the household of God. (Ephesians 2:19) "The spirit itself beareth witness with our spirit that we are the children of God and if children then heirs. Heirs of God and joint heirs with Christ. If so be that we suffer with Him that we may also be glorified together for I reckon that the sufferings of this present time are not worthy to be compared with the glory which shall be revealed in us." (Romans 8:16-18) "I saw a new heaven and a new earth: for the first heaven and the first earth were past away; and there was no more sea. And I, John, saw the holy city, new Jerusalem, coming down from God out of heaven, prepared as a bride adorned for her husband. And I heard a great voice out of heavens saying, Behold, the tabernacle of God is with men, and He will dwell with them, and they shall be His people, and God Himself shall be with them, and be their God. God shall wipe away all tears from their eyes; and there shall be no more death, neither sorrow, nor crying, neither shall there be any more pain: for the former things are passed away. And He that sat upon the throne said, Behold I make all things new." (Revelation 21:1-5) "And the Spirit and the bride say, Come. And let him that heareth say, Come. And let him that is athirst come. And whosoever will, let him take the water of life freely. Surely I come quickly. Amen. Even so, come, Lord Jesus. The grace of our Lord Jesus Christ be with you all. Amen. (Revelation 22:17,20-21)

Boycott shooting:

By Rich Mkhondo

A Kagiso youth died from bullet wounds at Baragwanath Hospital yesterday after an incident in which a businessman allegedly fired at a crowd which confronted him during a "consumer boycott monitoring routine".

A Krugersdorp Consumer Boycott Committee spokesman said Mr Angie Manganyine (19) was wounded when the businessman fired shots as the youths tried to stop him at the entrance to the township.

Mr Manganyine was rushed to hospital, where he died yesterday morning.

A police spokesman said the businessman was forci...

stopped at the entrance township by a group of y

He said: "They assa and removed clothin back of his car. He arm and fired shot youth.

"He is license arm. He repo the police. I man died l bullet wo

Swapo wil uit ambië aanval

YEX — Die Ve le in Suidwes bre naome Swapo die uit Zam wy Zuid George

Angiese regering in a militêre optrede in t tai het golf verdamp mak...

Urban terror increase dramatically in SA

**By Gary van Staden,
Political Reporter**

During the past 11 weeks a total of 25 explosive devices ranging from RPG rockets, limpet mines and landmines have been detonated in South Africa in an unprecedented wave of urban insurgency.

A total of 10 people have died

ca during 1985 — 150 pe more than last year and a double the previous highes of 55 in 1981.

Of the about 370 bomb sions in South Africa since more than 20 percent have in the Durban area.

Since the end of Septe Durban and its surrou areas have been rocked

killed in blas

Violence: Views cannot be giver

Staff Reporter

BECAUSE of the emergency regulations, the Cape Times cannot publish how Old Crossroads community and religious leaders view the causes of the violence and destruction which swept through their areas recently.

A Cape Times team and other representatives escorted by secu

that it "can you with le Later the could use ries.

Co me olice

Own Correspondent

Dur

Three people — all understood to be small children — were killed in a blast which ripped through a shop crowded with Christmas buyers i manzimtoti Sanlam Shopping Centre today. About another 14 were inj

ice units rushed to the scene of the blast and policeman with dogs batt he crowds.

Hospital in Durban was put on alert and reported to be standing by

10 stabbed to death in Soweto

Moutse: two die in violenc

Simmering discontent at the proposed

th shot after mourners clas

Police open fir

At Crossroads, battling by rival black factions left 65,000 homeless

SOUTH AFRICA

The Boot Comes Down

Emergency rule declared

[President Reagan] sits there like the great, big white chief of old ... The West, for my part, can go to hell

—ARCHBISHOP-ELECT DESMOND TUTU

Bomb blast death toll' climbs to

Nine injured in Jo'burg

from last October to January this year and was going to travel to Japan "but I strongly felt God leading me back here", said the 45-year-old preacher who has written 11 books, one about his travels on foot.

He began his career as a "street minister" among the drug addicts on Sunset Strip, Hollywood, but in 1969, at Christmas, he felt the call of God to "walk and

American pilgrim and son fasting for peace

Daily News Reporter

A MODERN-DAY pilgrim, who has carried a cross around the world for 17 years, started a seven-day fast in Durban's Town Gardens yesterday for peace and reconciliation in strife-torn South Africa.

It's just faith, says pilgrim after 16 years on the road

Daily News Reporter

SOME people think he is crazy, but for Arthur Blessitt his pilgrimage is just a matter of simple faith.

For 16 years he has been walking the world carrying a cross and handing out stickers printed with Christian messages.

He arrived in South Africa recently and he walked the Durban

mission to put the world on a path of peace

Carrying his cross on pilgrimage of peace

Hollywood with the cross on his back on

through 75

Arthur, fasting and praying in Oppenheimer Park
Johannesburg

Prayer for South Africa

Citizens and soldiers of Sumter ? at Arthur in Johannesburg

All God's children

Arthur and Wendy McDonald with Lindi Mangaliso, cousin

Reverend Allan Boesak
President of the World Council of Reformed Churches
and the Head of the United Democratic Front

hief Buthelezi, the Chief Minister to 8 million Zulus

Thou Art a Flower to Me

Words and Music by
Arthur Blessitt

Thou Art a Flower to Me

Words and Music by
ARTHUR BLESSITT

1. "Thou art a flow'r to me," spoke the man from
(2.) heart may fear, death's cold

Cal - va - ry; His crim - son blood that day
chills draw near. Some things I don't un - der-stand,

wash'd all my sins a - way. It was His
don't know the rea - son why. But in His

love for me that gave new life to me.
grace I trust. I know He'll hold my hand

That's why I shout and sing a - long my
un - til that day real soon, I'll see His

way.
face.

1.
2. Some - times my

2.

Millions Are Rising

by

Arthur Blessitt

Millions Are Rising

Words and Music by
ARTHUR BLESSITT

heav - en,_____ our hearts filled with love._____

___ Our feet, they are march - ing,_____ bring - ing good

news._____ Our hearts filled with joy, our hearts filled with

praise. Hal - le - lu - ia!

1 - <u>Arthur, A Pilgrim</u> (Book)
    One Man's Pilgrimage on Foot Around the World

2 - <u>Arthur Blessitt Street University</u> (Book)
    A practical teaching on how to witness to the lost.

3 - <u>Arthur Blessitt Street University</u> (6 cassette tape
    packet)

4 - <u>Arthur Blessitt Street University</u> (5 one hour VHS
     Videos)

5 - <u>Jesus Stickers</u> (Small 2 inch size)

6 - <u>Jesus Stickers</u> (Large 6 inch size)

7 - <u>Big Question</u> (Gospel pamphlet to use in witnessing)

8 - <u>New Life</u> (Pamphlet for new convert follow-up)

9 - <u>Arthur Blessitt Sheet Music</u>
          A. Thou Art A Flower To Me
          B. Millions Are Rising
          C. Drinking Wine, Feeling Fine, and Blowing My Mind
          D. I Sure Would Like To See You Again

10 - <u>If the Foundations Be Destroyed</u> (Book)
     by O. S. Hawkins, Studies in Jude

11 - <u>Postcard photograph</u> of Arthur Blessitt and his Scuba-
     diving and book publishing buddy - B.G. "Pete" Cantrell
     of Ada, Oklahoma
                    Order Form on Next Page

BLESSITT PUBLISHING

Order Form

	Quantity	Price	Total

Arthur,

Peacemaker .... _____ ...... $5.00 ... _____

Arthur, A Pilgrim .... _____ ...... $5.00 ... _____

Street Univ. - Book .... _____ ...... $5.00 ... _____

Street Univ. - Cassettes ..... _____ ..... $35.00 ... _____

Street Univ. - VHS Videos .... _____ .... $200.00 ... _____

Jesus Stickers (2") - 1,000 .. _____ ..... $15.00 ... _____

Jesus Stickers (6") - each ... _____ .... .25 ... _____

Big Question - Tract - 100 ... _____ ...... $3.00 ... _____

New Life - Tract - 100 .... _____ ...... $5.00 ... _____

Sheet Music - A (each sheet) . _____ ...... $2.50 ... _____

           - B (each sheet) . _____ .... 2.50 ... _____

           - C (each sheet) . _____ .... 2.50 ... _____

           - D (each sheet) . _____ .... 2.50 ... _____

If the Foundations Be Destroyed _____ ...... $6.00 ... _____

Postcard (Arthur and Pete) .. _____ .... 1.00 ... _____

Less 10% Discount with this page enclosed   _____

                                     Subtotal   _____

Ministry Support .... _____

                              Grand Total   _____

Check or Money Order payable to:

        Arthur Blessitt Evangelistic Association

        P.O. Box 69544

        Hollywood, CA   90069   U.S.A.